# Using Conflict Theo

Human conflict – from family feuds, to labor strikes, to international warfare – is an ever present and universal social problem, and the methods to manage it are a challenge for everyone, from average citizens to policy makers and social theorists. *Using Conflict Theory* will educate students about how, under what conditions, and why conflict erupts, and how it can be managed. It is a unique classroom book blending theory and practical application and for students the first to bridge the science of social theory and the art of practice.

The authors extract from classical sociological theory (Marx, Dahrendorf, Weber, Durkheim, and Parsons) and interpret for the student how these theoretical perspectives have contributed to understanding social conflict (its sources, the causes of escalation and deescalation of violence, the negotiations process). The perspectives of contemporary theorists (such as Randall Collins, James Coleman, Joseph Himes, and Hubert Blalock) are also brought to bear on these questions.

Sections on theory are followed by sections applying the theory to actual cases of social conflict, such as the American civil rights movement of the 1960s and the more recent conflict in Bosnia. The cases in these chapters and the contemporary examples that appear throughout the book can be used and easily adapted for discussion in the classroom or community setting. The book features useful, simple graphs, explaining formal theories of conflict, as well as strategies and methods to illustrate how theory is used by practitioners in negotiation and mediation.

The book is designed for classroom use in sociology, politics, international relations, peace studies, and other courses dealing with conflict, change, and social justice. Students will learn to understand conflict dynamics and to develop their own informed idea of how to deal constructively with any conflict they might have to analyze or face in real life.

Otomar J. Bartos is Professor Emeritus in the Department of Sociology at the University of Colorado. His publications dealing with conflict include *Process and Outcome of Negotiations*.

Paul Wehr is Associate Professor of Sociology at the University of Colorado at Boulder, where he cofounded the Conflict Research Consortium and heads the Peace and Conflict Studies program. He is the author of *Conflict Regulation*.

# Using Conflict Theory

Otomar J. Bartos
*University of Colorado at Boulder*

Paul Wehr
*University of Colorado at Boulder*

CAMBRIDGE
UNIVERSITY PRESS

PUBLISHED BY THE PRESS SYNDICATE OF THE UNIVERSITY OF CAMBRIDGE
The Pitt Building, Trumpington Street, Cambridge, United Kingdom

CAMBRIDGE UNIVERSITY PRESS
The Edinburgh Building, Cambridge CB2 2RU, UK
40 West 20th Street, New York, NY 10011-4211, USA
477 Williamstown Road, Port Melbourne, VIC 3207, Australia
Ruiz de Alarcón 13, 28014 Madrid, Spain
Dock House, The Waterfront, Cape Town 8001, South Africa

http://www.cambridge.org

First published 2002

Printed in the United States of America

*Typeface* ITC New Baskerville 10/13 pt      *System* LaTeX $2_\varepsilon$   [TB]

*A catalog record for this book is available from the British Library.*

*Library of Congress Cataloging in Publication data*
Bartos, Otomar J.
  Using conflict theory / Otomar J. Bartos, Paul Wehr.
    p.   cm.
  Includes bibliographical references and index.
  ISBN 0-521-79116-2 – ISBN 0-521-79446-3 (pbk.)
    1. Social conflict.   2. Social sciences – Philosophy.   I. Wehr, Paul
  Ernest, 1937–   II. Title.
  HM1121 .B37   2001        2001043151
  303.6 – dc21

ISBN 0 521 79116 2 hardback
ISBN 0 521 79446 3 paperback

To Linnycheck

*– O.J.B.*

To Christiane

*– P.W.*

# Contents

# Figures and Tables

**Figures**

## Tables

# Acknowledgments

THIS BOOK is a result of years of teaching and research. Many thanks are due our students whose comments and ideas helped us separate the important from the trivial, the certain from the dubious. We also thank the University of Colorado for a facilitating grant, our colleagues, the Department of Sociology, and Nancy Mann, Senior Instructor with the Editing Service of University of Colorado's Writing Program, for her editorial work on our manuscript. We owe much to our spouses for their encouragement and support. Finally, we are indebted to each other for patience, trust, and good humor, all essential for conflict moderation and productive behavior.

# CHAPTER ONE

# Introduction

IN THE twentieth century, knowledge about social conflict has increased considerably,[1] but so has the technology and scope of violence. As the new millennium begins, conflict actors must learn not only how to deescalate destructive conflicts, but also how to utilize "constructive" conflicts: how to clarify their own goals; how to select conflict strategies and tactics rationally; and how to apply them to achieve their goals while minimizing the costs.

## The Development of Conflict Knowledge

*Homo sapiens* has been learning about conflict throughout its development. That knowledge is spread across humanity, residing wherever humans live, work, and play. It is folk knowledge, used continuously in everyday life – in commerce, family relations, government, sport, child rearing. The ways of dealing with human conflict around the world are legion. They are passed down from parent to child, from generation to generation. They are transmitted from one life experience to the next. That knowledge is created within generations, as humans learn better how to interact with minimal cost. We do this pretty much unconsciously. Handling conflict is simply one of the life skills we learn and practice. Some of us do it better than others.

Particularly in the twentieth century we have become more conscious of how to understand conflict and how to deal with it in constructive ways. Conducted in numerous abstract and formal ways – through writing and teaching in schools and universities, and through research programs, seminars, and training – this effort was not simply due to curiosity but was a search for a solution to an increasingly serious problem, the growing scale and cost of human conflict. With each new wave of violent conflict in the world, there has been a renewed effort to understand it and control its harmful effects. We see a crisis-response pattern in these efforts.

The mounting wave of social conflict since 1800 (to pick a somewhat arbitrary date) can be traced to several developments: the growth of science and technology and its application to weaponry; the growth of the nation-state and its capacity to mobilize resources for control and violence; expanding populations. In fact, population pressure might be the leading cause of conflict increase, if one sees each human newborn as additional human need and thus conflict potential.

As conflict has steadily increased, so too has human effort to explain and manage it. The nineteenth century presented human society with problems that neither governments nor social theorists could ignore. The Napoleonic Wars and the revolutions of 1848 brought conflict and violence on a scale never before imagined. Napoleon had practiced total war, an institution so devastating in its consequences that in its wake, in 1815, Europe's governments created the Concert of Europe to prevent such unbridled interstate conflict in the future. The science and the art of diplomacy became the initial step in the human attempt to apply analysis and reason to managing conflict between nation-states.

Large-scale civil unrest was the second stimulus to the early development of conflict analysis and management. By the mid-nineteenth century, the industrial revolution had produced enormous demographic dislocations, extreme poverty, and a wide gulf between worker and owner. Karl Marx led a kind of conflict scholarship that produced credible and powerful analyses of conflict between classes. Marxist theory quickly became ideology as activists worked for political revolution to eliminate (as they thought and hoped) social conflict by restructuring economic and social relations.

In the late nineteenth century, ethnicity joined class as a focus of conflict scholarship. Powerful ethnic nationalism was being encouraged to serve various national and imperial policies. European governments were increasingly using ethnic identity and myths of racial superiority to carve out colonial empires on other continents. Within Europe itself, diverse ethnic groups artificially bound into nations were ever more restive. Writers like Georg Simmel theorized that intergroup conflict did not originate in instinctual urges but was a social process to be analyzed.

By 1900 huge areas of the world were controlled by the colonial powers of Europe. As a select few from the indigenous peoples in these areas were brought to the colonial capitals for European education, it was inevitable that conflict theory and practice then developing there would influence them. They would expand, reinvent, and apply it to liberate their people from colonial rule. They also had some earlier colonial rebels such as Simon Bolivar and Toussaint l'Ouverture as exemplars of liberation. One of the most interesting theoretical and practical challenges to colonialism was Gandhi's satyagraha approach, disciplined nonviolent resistance to domination. Gandhian conflict knowledge was unique in that it provided a means to struggle with one's oppressor without the spiraling violence and mutual harm that violent revolution produced. And satyagraha was to be applied not only to free India from Great Britain but to eliminate caste violence and religious communalism within India itself. Since Gandhi's death, the Gandhian movement has continued through the land gift (Bhoodan), self-help (Sarvodaya), and peace brigade (Shanti Sena) movements. The Gandhi Peace Foundation continues to study ways to apply his theory and method.

Gandhi himself had learned from the practice of the labor movement and from the theories of Marx and Thoreau that withholding one's cooperation through strikes and civil disobedience was a powerful method of struggle. In fact, industrial warfare became yet another major producer of conflict knowledge as the twentieth century unfolded. By the 1920s strikes and armed conflict between workers and owners were ever more common in the industrialized world. In the United States of the 1930s, an economic depression and a new government willing to intervene in industrial strife brought about collective bargaining. Federal law henceforth managed industrial conflict. Workers' rights to unionize and strike began to be protected through this procedure. The negotiation of contracts, review of grievances, and prevention of violence would all be regulated and monitored by the

Department of Labor and its newly created Mediation and Conciliation Service.

Collective bargaining stimulated a new area of conflict knowledge. Schools of industrial relations sprouted throughout the university world. Legions of skilled mediators and arbitrators emerged as industrial conflict was tamed. The American Arbitration Association, now a conflict management fixture in the United States, is another sign of expanding conflict knowledge. The Gandhian experience illustrates how conflict knowledge has been shared across cultures and societies. Gandhi, who had learned from Western theory and practice, gave back to the West what has become a creative and widely used method of dealing with conflict with minimal harm. In fact, the United Auto Workers in 1937 used a variation on the Gandhian theme in a sit-down strike against General Motors. Conflict knowledge had come full circle.

While theorists and practitioners in the West were learning how to moderate civil conflict, struggle between nations was intensifying. Twentieth-century technology and bureaucratic organization permitted states to take the methods of total war to new extremes. In two horrendous world conflicts, civilians were transformed from accidental victims of war into strategic targets. The culminating events in World War II – the incineration, vaporization, and extermination of millions of humans – evoked a new surge of intellectual and practical efforts to moderate conflict. With the introduction of nuclear weapons, the concept of total war took on a yet more ominous significance. The United Nations, peace research, and the peace movement were all examples of this new determination to understand and control international conflict. The Peace Research Institute in Oslo and the Center for Conflict Resolution at the University of Michigan were the first of a long line of academic centers to be established. Ultimately, even governments created their own programs, such as the United States Institute of Peace and the Stockholm International Peace Research Institute.

World War II ushered in a period of further political awakening and action among subject peoples. In the United States, African Americans created new forms of resistance to racial segregation and discrimination. But the civil rights movement of the 1950s and 1960s was only the first of several movements of liberation in the late twentieth century. Issues relating to gender, the natural environment, ethnicity, physical disability, and public policy all produced new pressure to invent mechanisms within communities for resolving conflict. The U.S. Department of Justice created the Community Relations Division to mediate interracial disputes. That office and the civil rights leaders' commitment to nonviolence contributed extensively to the largely peaceful desegregation of the South.

Liberation from colonial domination was occurring elsewhere in the world. As newly independent states appeared in Africa and Asia, civil conflict among ethnic and tribal groups required that new forms of international intervention be developed to moderate conflict. The policies of colonialism had ensured that civil conflict would occur in these new states. The European powers had carved up their colonial territories with little regard for the African political arrangements in place. Colonial boundaries often split ethnic groups in two, creating vulnerable minorities. Colonial authorities applied the "divide and rule" principle, using some peoples to control others.

In such arrangements intergroup resentments were bound to contribute to postindependence conflict. Departing colonial powers also added fuel by manipulating group against group in order to retain as much as possible of their economic investments. The departing colonials were soon replaced by the Cold War superpowers, the United States and the Soviet Union. Ideological allegiance, economic hegemony, and strategic and military influence stimulated civil wars in the developing world. Vietnam, Cambodia, Rwanda, Ethiopia, Angola, Somalia, and Zaire are prime examples of such residual conflicts. The United Nations has intervened to moderate many of these civil wars, developing successively peace keeping, peacemaking, and peace building as major additions to the body of conflict knowledge.

By the 1970s empowerment movements in the United States had greatly increased not only intergroup and interpersonal conflict but also conflict between individuals and organizations. More and more of this conflict was ending up in court, producing a court crisis of huge proportions. The response was a movement to facilitate out-of-court settlement of disputes. Alternative dispute resolution uses various third-party approaches – problem solving, mediation, arbitration – and has made its way into organizations, professions, and communities throughout the United States. Tens of thousands of persons have received formal training in mediation and other conflict management techniques. Several hundred peace and conflict studies programs in colleges and universities appeared in the 1970s and 1980s. Ombudsman offices and mediation services have been created in thousands of universities, school systems, and communities.

The possibility for learning more about conflict has motivated increasing numbers of people to develop personal conflict skills. Some use these professionally in law, public policy, family mediation, and the like. Others simply wish to create an informal peacemaker role for themselves. They act as neutral third parties in family disputes or neighborhood conflict, and as intervenors in international disputes (Wehr 1996). Citizen peace teams have been active in Nicaragua, Guatemala, Bosnia, Haiti, Sri Lanka, Iraq, and elsewhere.

In the nineteenth and twentieth centuries, then, there has been a series of conflict crises stimulating both practical and intellectual attempts to invent ideas and methods to deal with them. This book continues the effort to understand conflicts, both by discussing what humans actually do and by showing how conflicts can be approached more effectively and at less cost.

## Dealing with Conflict Economically and Effectively

Conflict and change are as inherent in the social world as order and permanence. Newton's physical law that each action produces a reaction has its counterpart in social theory. Kant and Hegel helped us to see that every individual, group, organization, or other unit in society represents a force whose action stimulates many counterforces. When force meets counterforce, either cooperation or conflict can result, depending on many factors. In either case, a new product or relationship (or synthesis, as Hegel would call it) emerges from the interaction. When the synthesis comes from conflict, the interaction is likely to be more costly and destructive than when it comes from cooperation. But, even then, conflict can be pursued and managed in less costly ways. Our ultimate objective is to identify some of the more economical ways of dealing with conflict. The greater the number of individuals, groups, organizations, and societies in conflict that are engaged constructively, the greater the development of human potential.

It is virtually impossible not to have beliefs and values about the role of conflict. Some may say that all conflict is destructive and thus to be avoided at all costs. But are there some conflicts that are beneficial to societies and individuals alike? We believe that conflict theory and practice based on it can be as useful for those dissatisfied with the status quo as for those who wish to keep things as they are. Too often, managing, reducing, and resolving conflict has simply deterred or postponed needed changes in power relations. In some cases, conflict management and reduction are the approach most productive of beneficial change; in other cases, it is best to escalate conflict and contest power.

This book assumes that wise and imaginative conflict action is basically the same for the individual as for the group or organization. After all, individuals represent the groups, organizations, categories, and societies of which they are members. So the principles of constructive conflict behavior that are explored in Chapters 9 and 10 apply across the levels of society. Although our three chapter-long illustrations (Chapters 4, 6, and 8) deal with conflicts between groups, we occasionally use shorter examples to show how the theory applies to individuals and organizations.

## Theorizing about Conflict

Out of the great diversity of conflict knowledge, it is possible to extract some fundamental insights that seem to hold true for all conflicts. To present them in an easily understandable manner, we will use two guiding principles: focus on general theories, and present these theories in a simplified way.

### Generality and Simplicity

The theories to be discussed are general, that is, applicable to many different types of conflict. For example, we assume that the civil war in Bosnia might be due to the same fundamental causes as the civil rights struggle in the United States: the desire to redistribute scarce resources, to enact incompatible roles, or to pursue incompatible values. Because most of the fundamental questions about conflicts were asked – and often answered – by the pioneers in the

**Figure 1.1.** A Causal Proposition

field, emphasis will be on the work of classical theoreticians such as Durkheim ([1893] 1964), Marx ([1894] 1967), Weber ([1922] 1947), and Simmel ([1908] 1955).

Once such general theories are identified, they are converted into simple causal statements that can be translated into diagrams. For example, much of the theory dealing with group solidarity can be summarized in the proposition "If the level of conflict solidarity within a group increases, the chances that it will engage in conflict behavior increase as well." (As we explain later, we are using conflict "behavior" as a general term that includes the more specific term conflict "action.") This proposition can be expressed graphically as shown in Figure 1.1. We should add that, occasionally, we might use terminology that does not use the word "cause." For example, instead of saying that injustice was a cause of the civil rights movement, we might say that one *reason* for the civil rights movement was injustice.

### Limitations of Our Approach

To a large extent, attempts to simplify the theories of the classical theorists are justifiable because their masterpieces are both works of science and works of art – and their scientific core can be distilled into simple causal statements. Still, this approach may offend some readers by omitting much of the genius of the masters. Another problem is that simplified theories omit some of the considerations mentioned by contemporary writers. For example, we do not include intervention by third parties as a part of our general theory, even though such interventions may affect the conflict in important ways.[2]

Moreover, we must forgo consideration of some influential theories, among them the so-called critical theory, a school of thought that owes much to Karl Marx. Its adherents advance several criticisms of contemporary societies and those who theorize about it. They argue that Marx is interpreted too mechanically, that positivism is flawed because it fails to see humans as true actors, that sociologists are too ready to accept the status quo, that the so-called instrumental rationality leads to technocratic thinking and, ultimately, to monstrosities such as Nazi concentration camps, that mass media create popular culture that is phony and repressive. They also advocate some remedies – for example, Marxists should pay more attention to the subjective aspects of human existence, societies must be studied in their totality, and the interrelationship of their parts must be understood (Ritzer 1992, 142–150).

Important as these considerations are, because they are not easily converted into causal propositions, they are not incorporated into the main body of our theory. At the same time, important aspects of critical theory that *can* be converted into causal statements about social conflict – Marx's theory of class struggle and Habermas's thesis that today the "system colonizes the lifeworld" – are considered here (see Chapter 3).

Thus this book should be viewed as only an introduction to conflict theory, one that deals just with the most important causes of conflict. Once readers have mastered the material presented here, they should broaden their understanding by reading more complex analyses of conflicts, such as that given by Kriesberg ([1973] 1982; 1998).

### Some Benefits

Once we have identified the *possible* causes of conflict behavior, we can explain why a particular conflict exists. For example, we argue that conflict behavior can occur for six main reasons: the parties may have (or believe that they have) incompatible goals, they each may have achieved high solidarity, they may have organized for conflict, they can mobilize their conflict resources, they may be hostile toward their opponents, and they may have sufficient material resources (see Figure 1.2).

In many conflicts only *some* of these causes are influential. Identifying the operative causes in any single conflict helps us both to understand that conflict and to deal with it. For example, if one concludes that a particular urban riot is driven primarily by hostility, one not only comes to understand that conflict but also obtains a basis for dealing with it: if one wishes to prevent future riots, one may attempt to lessen the hostility by addressing the rioters' valid grievances or

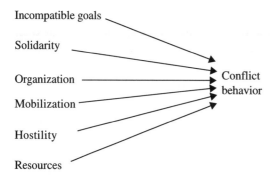

**Figure 1.2.** A Theory of Conflict Behavior

may ask the community leaders to call for calm and restraint; if one wishes to encourage more riots, one may try to increase the hostility by organizing rallies that emphasize past injustices and demonize the opponents.

Two main objectives guide the discussion in this book: to explain why conflicts start and develop in certain ways (Chapters 1–8), and to indicate how conflicts can be used constructively (Chapter 9). In the concluding chapter we summarize our theory and suggest how one might develop conflict skills further.

## Plan of the Book

Chapter 2 prepares the ground by considering some fundamental questions. What is a conflict? What is meant by goal incompatibility? What is hostility? What are the main types of conflict behavior?

Most of the subsequent chapters consider the main causes of social conflicts. Why do some groups have incompatible goals? Why do hidden disagreements erupt into open conflicts? What causes conflicts to escalate and deescalate? Each of these questions is treated in a set of two chapters: the first chapter in each set presents the theory that answers the question, the second applies the theory to a specific example. On occasion, the application chapter also outlines some principles useful to those who wish to deal with conflicts constructively.

Chapter 3 begins by considering the reasons why any two groups may develop incompatible goals. It argues that this nearly always happens because the parties contest certain resources, or because they play different roles, or because they are culturally different. The main resources will be the works of Marx, Dahrendorf, Durkheim, and Weber. Chapter 4 applies their theories to the struggle for civil rights in the United States. It concludes that the primary reason for the struggle has been that African Americans have not received their fair share of scarce resources (wealth, power, and prestige) and that many of them have lived in abject poverty.

Chapter 5 considers why a latent conflict becomes overt. It argues that incompatible goals are likely to lead to conflict behavior if "conflict groups" are formed. Among the conditions favoring their formation are not only incompatible goals but also high group solidarity and availability of resources. The theories of Homans and Dahrendorf are used to illustrate the role that solidarity plays in mobilizing for conflict. Chapter 6 applies these theories to a conflict over faculty tenure within a university. It concludes that the outbreak of that particular conflict was due to almost all of the possible causes.

Chapter 7 discusses the conditions that determine whether an overt conflict escalates or deescalates. As a formal model of conflict suggests, a conflict can escalate even when the adversaries' "inner" tendencies (to escalate unilaterally, to retaliate, and to express their hostility) remain unchanged. At the same time, these tendencies are bound to change over time, because of feedbacks from the conflict itself. When that happens, the conflict can escalate even further – or it can deescalate. Chapter 8 applies these theories to the Bosnian civil war.

Chapter 9 relates the principles of conflict management, such as those discussed by Deutsch (1973) and Fisher and Ury (1981), to the discussion in the preceding chapters. It explains why such principles are sound and how they can be applied to manage conflicts.

Chapter 10 reviews our theory and suggests how you can use it and certain specific skills to deal with conflicts. The book concludes with an appendix providing a more detailed historical account of the events discussed in Chapter 8, the war in Bosnia.

# CHAPTER TWO

# Understanding Conflict

IN THE 1880s ranchers in the western United States fought over water rights; in 1939 Germany attacked Poland; last week a husband and wife argued bitterly over their finances. That all were engaged in a conflict is obvious. In fact, it may seem that nothing is simpler than recognizing a conflict – after all, it involves fighting, does it not? Actually, no, not always. Some conflicts are "latent" and do not involve overt fighting; and some overt fights, such as wrestling matches, are not due to a conflict. Thus it is important to agree on what is and what is not a conflict.

## What Is a Conflict?

It might not surprise you to hear that even theoreticians differ in how they view conflict. For many practical purposes, they may understand it as a special set of interrelated elements: parties, issues, dynamics, and contexts. To gain a deeper understanding, however, they may use certain abstract concepts such as cause and effect; direct, indirect, and intervening causes; and payoff matrices. The discussion in this chapter deals with these concepts.

Students of social conflict have offered many different definitions of conflict. Early on, Park and Burgess defined it simply as struggle for status. Somewhat later, Mack and Snyder defined it as struggle not only for status but also for scarce resources and significant social change

(Himes 1980, 12). Other writers have offered additional definitions.[1] How then should we conceive of conflict?

We may begin by acknowledging that there is a good reason for the great variety of definitions. They tend to reflect authors' theoretical orientations: psychologists might define conflict in terms of the adversaries' inner states,[2] sociologists in terms of observable behavior,[3] and so on. The definition used here is similarly anchored in theory – our theory. That theory assumes that conflict can originate either in goal incompatibility or in hostility (or in both), and that it involves a unique type of behavior, conflict behavior. Thus conflict is defined here as a situation in which *actors use conflict behavior against each other to attain incompatible goals and/or to express their hostility.*

But, once again, this definition is more complex than you might think: the *actors* referred to in the definition can be not only individuals but also groups. This means that, at times, we speak about the "behavior" of groups, a practice that some scholars might find objectionable. Yet it preserves uniformity of terminology – after all, we view both individuals and groups as actors – as well as brevity. Moreover, it is common practice to refer to groups "acting." For example, we say that "In 1941, Japan launched an unprovoked attack against the United States" instead of saying, "In 1941, members of the Japanese government decided, without provocation, to send airplanes manned by Japanese pilots to attack Pearl Harbor."

The remaining three concepts used in the definition – *goal incompatibility, hostility,* and *conflict behavior* – are so important that they are discussed in detail in the following pages. Some additional conflict-related terms, such as violence, fairness, and negotiation, are considered later: the concepts of fairness and justice in Chapter 3; the concept of negotiation in Chapter 9. But two important – and controversial – distinctions can be considered now. We begin with the distinction between conflict and competition.

When several businesspeople bid for a contract, without engaging in conflict action such as spreading false rumors or making threats, they are in competition – but not conflict – with each other. In general, people who are in competition do not engage in conflict interaction and, in fact, may not even be aware that they are competing; they are always seeking the same end; and they usually seek what belongs to a third party rather than what belongs to the opponent

(Kriesberg [1973] 1982, 17). If, on the other hand, they *do* direct conflict behavior at each other, they are in a conflict. It should be added that some writers disagree, viewing competition as a special kind of conflict.

A second distinction that should be made is that between nonviolent and violent conflict. Let us illustrate the difference with the annual fall rut in a herd of elk. In the conflict over females, the males use several types of conflict action: threat postures, strength testing, snorting and bellowing, antler locking, even flight and pursuit. Yet rarely is real violence done in such combat, and then only unintentionally. Humans too use nonviolent conflict actions such as threat, flight, testing, and promise in their conflict – but, unlike male elk, they also do physical and psychological harm to one another. Thus the term "conflict action" will be used here to apply to both violent and nonviolent behavior.

## Incompatible Goals

It is often difficult to determine reliably whether goals are in fact incompatible. Two approaches are quite helpful. The first approach is something that probably occurs to you first: you ask whether it is logically impossible for both parties' goals to be achieved simultaneously.[4] For example, if workers in a factory wish to work as little as possible and be paid as much as possible, while the owners wish them to work as hard as possible for as little pay as possible, it is logically impossible for both goals to be reached simultaneously. Similarly, it is logically impossible for a wife and her husband each to have her or his way if the wife wishes to have children and the husband does not. It is impossible for both the Israelis and the Syrians to have exclusive sovereignty over the Golan Heights.

The second approach is more complex but theoretically more rewarding: you ask whether the two parties have incompatible "payoffs."[5]

### Using Payoff Matrices

To introduce matrix representation of conflict, consider an example. Suppose a husband does not want any children but his wife wants four. Suppose furthermore that you had a way to assess – perhaps through

Table 2.1. *Incompatible Interests of Wife and Husband*

|  | Conflict Parties | |
| --- | --- | --- |
|  | Husband | Wife |
| *Goals* | | |
| Four children | −3 | 10 |
| No children | 4 | −8 |

a questionnaire – how much each outcome is worth to each party and found that having four children was worth −3 points to the husband,[6] 10 points to the wife; and that having no children was worth 4 points to the husband, −8 points to the wife. This situation may be represented by the "payoff matrix" displayed in Table 2.1. Note that, in this table, the goals of each spouse are represented by a row that has a positive payoff for him (her): having no children is the husband's goal because it has for him the payoff of +4; having four children is the wife's goal because it has for her the payoff of +10.

When you face new terminology, you often need to stay alert to certain distinctions. In this case, you need to remember the difference between an alternative, its outcome, and its payoff. An *alternative* is one of the actions that the decision maker can choose from (such as having four children); an *outcome* comprises all the consequences of that action (such as feeling fulfilled, having less money and time for leisure activities, having less time with the spouse); and a *payoff* is the total value the decision maker assigns to the outcome (such as the +10 the wife presumably assigns to having four children). Note that a payoff matrix specifies explicitly only what the alternatives are (the rows of the matrix) and what the payoffs are (the numbers within the cells). The outcomes are left unspecified, and readers must use their imagination to fill them in.

Perhaps you are puzzled by the numbers that appear in Table 2.1. Although they are to a large extent arbitrary, they represent a fact of real life: that the importance people attach to various events varies. In this case, the wife values having four children highly, while devaluing the possibility of having no children; the husband's values are the opposite of hers, though less intense. This being the case, we conclude that the goals and the interests of the husband and wife are incompatible because when an event has a positive payoff for one of them, it always has a negative payoff for the other.

### Advantages of Matrix Representation

Payoff tables of the kind given in Table 2.1 have certain advantages. First, they permit us to identify incompatibility: *two* goals are incompatible if one has a positive payoff only for the party and the other only for the opponent. For example, Table 2.1 shows the goal of four children as incompatible with the goal of no children because the first goal has positive payoff only for the wife (+10), the other only for the husband (+4). Incidentally, we may say that *one* goal is "not mutually acceptable" if it has a positive payoff for only one side. Thus, in Table 2.1, having four children is not mutually acceptable because it has positive payoff only for the wife.

Second, using payoff matrices allows you to consider conflicts in which there are more than two alternatives under consideration. For example, suppose that you surveyed workers and managers in a factory and concluded that they have three main goals, and that the attractiveness of these goals can be represented by the payoffs shown in Table 2.2.[7] You will no doubt note that, while there are two incompatible goals (wage of $20 versus $10), there is also a third goal, the solvency of the firm, that is shared by both parties (i.e., that has positive payoff for both sides).

Table 2.2. *Incompatible and Compatible Goals of Workers and Managers*

|  | Conflict Parties | |
|---|---|---|
|  | Workers | Managers |
| *Goals* | | |
| Wage: $20 per hour | 7 | −3 |
| Wage: $10 per hour | −4 | 8 |
| Solvency of the firm | 2 | 5 |

Table 2.3. *An Example of a Zero-Sum Conflict*

|  | Conflict Parties | |
|---|---|---|
|  | Husband | Wife |
| *Goals* | | |
| Four children | −10 | 10 |
| No children | 8 | −8 |

A third advantage might not seem to be very important, but it is to a theoretician: payoff matrices allow him or her to distinguish between goals and interests. The *goals* of a party are quite specific: they are the alternatives that have a positive payoff for the party.[8] Thus Table 2.2 specifies that the workers have two goals, the wage of $20 and the solvency of the firm; the managers also have two goals, the wage of $10 and the solvency of the firm. The *interests* of a party are more diffuse: they are all the outcomes from all possible alternatives that have positive payoffs for the party. Because certain desired outcomes – such as security, recognition, respect, and justice – seem to be universal, they are sometimes viewed as the party's "true" interests. As we discuss shortly, interests are incompatible if, in general, they are negatively correlated: when the party's payoff for an outcome is high, the payoff of the opponent tends to be low.

Fourth, payoff representation allows you to determine the *extent* to which the goals and interests are incompatible. In the example of Table 2.1, the payoffs of the husband and wife, although divergent, are not totally incompatible. They could be, for example, exactly opposite for the two parties, as shown in Table 2.3. Incidentally, you now know that the often-used term "zero-sum game" corresponds to an extreme conflict and that it can be represented by a matrix in which each row sums up to zero.

Fifth, matrix representation of payoffs in a conflict allows us to determine whether *an agreement is possible*. For example, because in the case represented by Table 2.2 "solvency of the firm" has a positive payoff for both adversaries, the workers and the managers could begin their negotiation by agreeing to pursue this goal. It is also possible to determine whether a compromise is possible on something about which the parties do not agree. One possible solution is to "split the difference," giving the workers a wage that is halfway between what they demand ($20) and what the management is willing to pay ($10), that is, a wage of $15.

To determine whether this compromise is acceptable to the two parties, we must compute the payoffs (rather than wages) associated with it. It turns out that this can be accomplished by performing the following computations (see Bartos 1967):

Workers' payoff: $.50 * (7) + .50 * (-4) = 1.5$
Management's payoff: $.50 * (-3) + .50 * (8) = 2.5$

Because the resulting "compromise" payoffs (1.5 for the workers and 2.5 for the managers) are positive for both sides, this 50–50 split is acceptable to both.

Finally, matrix representation allows you to determine what agreement is "best" for both sides. In our example, a strong argument can be made that the wage corresponding to the 50–50 split ($15) is close to being best: it can be shown that it is even better to agree on a wage that is only slightly higher, $15.46. If you are willing to go through a fairly technical discussion, you can learn why this wage is best by reading about the so-called Nash solution (Nash 1950; Luce and Raiffa 1967; Bartos 1967).

### Identifying Goals and Interests

The practical consequence of this discussion is that you can benefit from both the concept of logical contradiction and the concept of payoff matrix. To illustrate, suppose that one country invades another. How do you determine whether the goals and interests of the two countries involved in the conflict action are incompatible?

First, you ask whether each country claims sovereignty over the same territory, as do both Israelis and Palestinians over East Jerusalem. If both do, then, since sovereignty means exclusive control, it is *logically* impossible for either of them to claim sovereignty over the territory and accept its occupation by the opponent. Second, you try to obtain a rough estimate of the payoffs. True, it is seldom possible to assign exact payoffs in real-world conflicts. Still, if each party is "vitally interested" in the territory, you may assume that each assigns high positive payoffs to its own occupation of it and very low negative payoffs to its occupation by the opponent. You may also try to guess the payoffs for additional alternatives, such as assigning each country only a part of the territory, or having the territory administered by a neutral body. This helps you to determine whether an agreement can be reached.

Thus you can gain considerable insight into any conflict if you keep in mind the matrix approach. You then can determine what the main alternatives are; speculate on the likely consequences of each alternative; and guess whether a party assigns high, low, or negative payoffs to these consequences.

## Hostility

The definition of conflict offered here implies that conflict behavior can occur not only because the parties have incompatible goals but also because they feel hostility toward each other. Whether you rely on your intuitive understanding of hostility or on a more formal definition such as an "antagonism, opposition, or resistance in thought or principle" (*Webster's* 1976, 553), you undoubtedly realize that hostility plays quite a different role in conflict than do incompatible goals. The distinction between rational and nonrational behavior helps us to understand this difference.

### *Rational Behavior*

During the Cuban missile crisis of 1962, the United States and the Soviet Union came close to war. Soviet Premier Krushchev decided to challenge U.S. missile supremacy by secretly installing medium-range missiles in Cuba. Informed about this, President Kennedy faced a crucial decision: if the United States responded too strongly, a nuclear war might result; if he responded too weakly, the influence of the Soviet Union would increase. During lengthy cabinet meetings, several options were considered, ranging from invading Cuba and destroying the missile sites to registering a strong protest and demanding the removal of the missiles. After listening to arguments from his aides for and against each option, Kennedy decided on an action that was neither too provocative nor too submissive: he ordered the U.S. Navy to start a blockade of Cuba, inspecting Soviet ships to determine whether they carried missile-related cargo. At the same time, he started a personal dialogue with Krushchev, informing him of the impending blockade. For a while, the Soviets did not respond, and two of their ships proceeded toward Cuba, protected by a submarine. As the ships were approaching the 500-mile barrier imposed by the United States, confrontation appeared inevitable. But, to the Americans' huge relief, the Russian ships stopped before crossing the barrier, and intense negotiations ensued. A compromise was worked out: the Soviets agreed to withdraw their missiles; the United States agreed not to invade Cuba and to withdraw American missiles from Turkey (Kennedy 1969).

In most important respects, Kennedy's decision-making process was "rational," because he reached his decision through lengthy deliberation during which he (1) considered a number of possible actions, (2) considered the likely consequences of each action, (3) evaluated each set of consequences, and (4) chose the action with the most desirable consequences.

Given the fact that payoff matrices play an important role in the theory of rational decision making,[9] it is not surprising that there is a close parallel between these steps and the steps involved in constructing a payoff matrix. To construct a payoff matrix and use it rationally, you must:

1. Determine the possible alternatives.
2. Determine the outcomes associated with each alternative.
3. Assign a payoff to each outcome.
4. Choose the alternative with the highest payoff.

Some theoreticians – notably Weber ([1922] 1947) – argue that we should distinguish between two types of rationality. One of these is the "instrumental" rationality. It occurs when your action is directed at a *specific goal* that can be obtained, such as the best way to avoid rush hour traffic, buying the best car with the money you have, or deciding whether you should study in order to pass tomorrow's examination or can afford to go to a party. The other type is "value" rationality. It occurs when your objective is to conform to a *vaguely defined set of values*, such as when a Catholic is trying to decide which of several possible alternatives – making a contribution to her church, going to confession, and so on – might be the most appropriate behavior.

Although the abstract principles guiding rational actions are clear, their practical implementation is fraught with difficulties, because different individuals, faced with the same situation, may differ in what action they see as rational: they might consider a different set of alternatives, have different beliefs about what outcomes are likely, or evaluate the outcomes differently. For example, had Kennedy not considered a blockade as a feasible alternative, he might have opted for invading Cuba; had Krushchev foreseen correctly how Kennedy would react, he might have chosen not to install the missiles; had Krushchev not considered the inferior power of the Soviet Union unacceptable, he might have chosen not to act the way he did.

Despite these complications, one can draw a clear (abstract) distinction between rational and nonrational action. An action is (objectively) rational if it is reached by an actor who not only followed the steps outlined here but did it with an almost supernatural skill: he or she considered a set of all relevant alternatives, assessed their outcomes correctly, evaluated them in accordance with his or her values (or the values of the group he or she represents), and then chose the action that was the best. An action is (objectively) nonrational if it is not best (not highest-valued) in this sense.

## Hostility as Nonrational Behavior

When we are angry, we often act contrary to our better judgment – that is, we act nonrationally. Most acts driven by emotions such as anger tend to be spontaneous and quick, and often at odds with what a more careful deliberation might suggest. For example, a husband and a wife, after spending hours deciding where to go for their vacation, may finally reach a compromise accepted by both. And then, when it is time to make reservations, one of the pair may say, "I really do not want to do this; I hate that place." It does not help for the other person to say, "But you agreed!" because the reluctant partner may simply answer, "I know, but I do not feel like doing it."

The main reason why rational and emotional actions are often at odds is that whereas rational action takes into account all of the possible consequences, emotional action does not. When I am angry, I need to strike out at somebody, and damn the consequences. Thus feelings – especially feelings of hostility – are often an obstacle to settling a conflict and implementing the settlement. A skillful mediator is well aware of this fact and works hard to remove this obstacle. Validating hostility and allowing it to express itself in harmless ways are among the tools that help this process.

In a conflict, the most important emotion is hostility toward the enemy. Thus Kennedy, instead of engaging in careful deliberation, might have responded impulsively and ordered immediate invasion of Cuba. In some cases, a conflict may start rationally, only to deteriorate into nonrationality. Thus while a demonstration may have been planned as a disciplined way of letting one's point of view be known, it may turn into a riot that is fueled by hatred, expressed in rock throwing, burning of cars, looting, and even killing. Similarly, reasonable efforts by police to maintain order may be transformed into a "police riot" if they are carried away by hostile emotions toward the demonstrators. Such was the case in the Chicago demonstrations in the summer of 1968.

The relationship between hostility and conflict behavior is complex. On the one hand, hostility adds fuel to and intensifies conflict behavior. On the other hand, conflict also intensifies hostility: as conflict continues and the parties inflict injuries on each other, the participants are no longer motivated solely by a desire to reach their original goals; increasingly, they become determined to destroy the enemy. The nature of conflict is thus transformed.

## Conflict Action

Conflict has been defined here as "a situation in which actors use conflict behavior against each other to attain incompatible goals and/or to express their hostility." But what is – and what is not – "conflict behavior"? To most of us, this term evokes images of fighting, violence, coercion, and force. But our definition of conflict suggests that conflict behavior is *any* behavior that helps the party to achieve its goal that is incompatible with that of the opponent or that expresses its hostility toward him or her.

Social scientists are sometimes accused of using obscure language to express relatively simple ideas. In some cases, we must plead guilty. But some technical terms are essential if you wish to understand conflict. One pair of useful terms is conflict action and conflict behavior. We speak about participants' conflict "action" when we are assuming that they are guided by rational considerations; when we assume that they may be rational *or* nonrational, we use the term conflict "behavior." For example, we might say that demonstrators are engaged in conflict *action* when they march through a city in a planned fashion, using signs and nonviolent language to demand the ouster of a crooked politician. When such intent and planning may be absent, we might use a more general term conflict *behavior.* This distinction is not hard and fast, but, because we hope to show how to approach conflict in a thoughtful manner, we use, most of the time, the term conflict action.

Another important distinction is between "coercive" and "noncoercive" action (behavior). This distinction is so important that we give it special attention later. You should know, however, that some writers use the terms "competitive" and "cooperative" instead.[10] We prefer our terminology because it captures an essential point: a conflict is quite different when the adversaries use force than when they don't.

### Coercive Action

Coercion forces the opponents to do what they do not wish to do. It accomplishes this by threatening to inflict injury on them, or by actually inflicting it (Kriesberg [1973] 1982, 116). The distinction between threatening and actually inflicting injury is necessary because the two have theoretically different interpretations: while the threat of injury is best conceived within the framework of a payoff matrix, the actual injury is not.

*Actual Coercion.* We use "actual" coercion if we try to weaken our opponents by injuring them. It is useful to distinguish between physical violence and symbolic injury. Severe *physical* injury can be violent: hurting or killing the opponents, or destroying their property (Himes 1980, 103). For example, soldiers of one nation try to kill those of another, or boys fighting in a schoolyard try to knock each other down. Or physical injury can be nonviolent, such as depriving the opponents of resources they need. For example, a nation may punish its opponent by preventing ships from going in or out of its harbors, or a wife may lock her husband out of their house. *Symbolic* injury, on the other hand, weakens the opponent by inducing fear, shame, or guilt through actions such as jeering or using derogatory names. For example, strikers may

Table 2.4. *A Revised Version of a*
*Husband-Wife Conflict*

|  | Conflict Parties | |
| --- | --- | --- |
|  | Husband | Wife |
| *Goals* | | |
| Four children | −3 | 10 |
| No children | 4−10 = −6 | −8 |

try to dissuade nonunion workers from entering a factory by calling
them "scabs."

*Threat of Coercion.* The primary consequence of an actual injury is
to decrease the opponents' ability to continue the conflict. Thus it
should not be viewed as involving a change in their payoffs. A threat of
violence, on the other hand, is best understood within the framework
of payoff matrices: if the opponents' payoffs for their original goal are
sufficiently reduced by the threat, they will abandon it and may adopt
the threatening party's goal.

Let us illustrate using the conflict between husband and wife, represented in Table 2.2. Suppose that the wife threatens to leave her husband if he does not agree to have four children, and that this threat
is believed by the husband.[11] Moreover, the wife's leaving would be
so devastating to him that the threat decreases his payoff for having
no children by 10 points (see Table 2.4). Because now his payoff for
"four children" is higher (−3) than the payoff for "no children" (−6),
a rational husband who does not have any other choice will agree to
having four children. But he has been coerced into choosing an option that has negative payoff for him, that is, he will do something he
does not want to do[12] – which, incidentally, suggests why threats are
often a bad strategy: when a person is forced to choose an option with
a negative payoff, he or she is bound to feel hostile and will be less
likely to cooperate in the future.

Although the distinction between threatening and actually inflicting an injury is conceptually clear, in practice the two are often inter-
twined and hard to separate. For example, consider two men who have
been fighting until one of them gives up. How should we interpret the

defeated man's actions? Should we assume that he no longer views fighting as profitable, or should we assume that he is no longer capable of fighting? Another complication is that threats do more than make resistance less desirable. As we discuss in Chapter 8, threats may increase the opponents' hostility and thus make them less likely to yield.

### Noncoercive Conflict Action

Not all conflict actions involve coercion. Some, such as joint searching for new options, involve "pure" cooperation. Others, such as persuasion and rewarding, lie somewhere between full-scale coercion and pure cooperation: they resemble coercion in that their objective is to make the opponent accept the player's goal; they resemble pure cooperation in that they use inducements rather than force.

*Persuasion.* Like a threat of coercion, persuasion works by changing the payoffs that the goals offer to the opponents. But while threat of coercion decreases the payoff for one's opponents' original goal, persuasion increases their payoff for the party's own goal. It does so at no cost to itself, simply by bringing to the opponents' attention certain favorable outcomes they had originally not considered. For example, suppose that parents want their son to go to college, but he does not wish to go. They can try to persuade him by pointing out that, if he goes to college, he will be able to make new friends, enjoy sports, and take interesting courses. If he does not go to college, he will have to find employment immediately. And surely that would not be as pleasant as college life.

Note that successful persuasion seldom involves abstract logical arguments or righteous positioning. Instead, it involves showing one's opponents that it is to *their* advantage to adopt "our" goals. Thus a pro-choice advocate, trying to persuade a pro-life advocate to change her action should not argue that his point of view is morally right; instead, he should point out that the pro-life advocate could herself have an unwanted or high-risk pregnancy, that an abortion performed under medical supervision would save her from having to raise an unwanted child, or might even save her life.

*Promising a Reward.* Another type of conflict action involves promising rewards. Those who promise a reward also play to the opponent's self-interest, but instead of emphasizing existing options the opponent has overlooked, they create – usually at their own expense – new outcomes that are rewarding for the opponent.[13] In the parlance of the theory of games, they create "side payments" that is, a commitment to reward their opponents if they accept the first party's goals. Thus the parents may try to induce their son to go to college by promising to buy him a new car to take him there.

*Pure Cooperation.* What may be called "pure" cooperation differs from the actions discussed so far in that its objective is to find a solution that is gratifying to both parties. Usually, it involves searching for a goal that is different from those the parties had originally pursued. In some cases, each party searches for such a solution on its own; in other cases, the search itself is a joint one, involving a continuing dialogue. Some cooperative actions are preparatory to finding such a solution. For example, a party may try to understand its opponents' point of view; it may attempt to validate that point of view; or it may seek third-party assistance in resolving the conflict. We consider such cooperative actions here and in the coming chapters and devote Chapter 9 exclusively to them.

### Degree of Coerciveness

For many purposes it is important to consider the specific types of action described thus far. But for other purposes – such as making causal statements of the form "An increase in X leads to an increase to Y" – it is necessary to have a term that refers to the "degree" of a conflict, terms like intensity, destructiveness, or strength. There does not seem to be a word that captures this perfectly, but the term "coerciveness" seems quite appropriate. For example, when two boys start to hit each other after merely exchanging sarcastic remarks, it may be said that their behavior becomes more coercive.

Figure 2.1 shows that our use of the term "degree of coerciveness" runs into a slight conceptual problem: we identify the lower end of the continuum both as corresponding to (a low level of) coerciveness

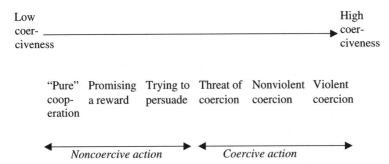

**Figure 2.1.** Coerciveness of Conflict Action

and to "noncoercive action." How can something be both coercive and *non*coercive? We ask the reader to bear with us, recognizing that this problem is often encountered when one tries to convert a continuum into a concept with only two categories.[14]

In general, it is possible to arrange the different types of conflict action on a continuum from low to high degree of coerciveness, as shown in Figure 2.1. "Pure cooperation" is an action that is minimally coercive: while inducing the opponent to abandon his original goal, it takes his interests as much into account as those of the actor herself. "Promising reward" is somewhat more coercive: although it rewards the opponent, it does so only in order to promote the actor's own interests. "Trying to persuade" is even more coercive: it pursues the actor's own interests without rewarding the opponent's in any way; it merely notes which of his interests coincide with those of the actor. The remaining three benchmarks – threats, nonviolent coerciveness, and violent coerciveness – clearly manifest increasing coerciveness: "threat of coercion" because it decreases the opponent's payoffs; "nonviolent coerciveness" because it is punishing to the opponent; and "violent coerciveness" because it is highly punishing, possibly even fatal, to the opponent.

## Conclusions

Although the very concept of conflict is the subject of considerable controversy, the theories to be discussed in subsequent chapters suggest a fairly simple definition: conflict is a situation in which actors use conflict action against each other to attain incompatible goals and/or to express their hostility. To make this definition meaningful, one must understand its three main terms: incompatible goals, hostility, and conflict behavior. The term "incompatible goals" invites several questions. What is meant by incompatibility? What is a goal, and how does it differ from an "interest"? Is it possible to have different degrees of incompatibility? How can one identify a goal that is acceptable to both sides? A goal that is best for both? So-called payoff matrices help one to answer these questions.

Much could be said about hostility, but to understand the unique role it plays in conflicts, consider its nonrational aspects. Unlike rational action (which is based on careful deliberation and uses a specific procedure of judgment and valuing), expressions of hostility are nonrational in that they are quick, impulsive, and often at odds with what action a rational analysis might suggest. Thus conflict behavior that is heavily influenced by hostility is often damaging to the actor's own long-range interests.

"Conflict behavior" is an umbrella term that covers many diverse types of behavior. It refers to (more or less) rational action as well as to (nonrational) expressions of hostilities; to behavior that is highly coercive (such as physically harming the opponent) as well as to behavior that is fully cooperative (such as searching for a mutually acceptable solution). Still, it is desirable to have a concept that treats these qualitative differences as matters of degree – and the concept of coerciveness is such a concept (see Figure 2.1).

# CHAPTER THREE

# Development of Incompatible Goals

MUCH OF this book is about understanding social conflicts. Why did World War II occur? Why do I and my husband fight so often over trivial matters? Why does the Palestinian conflict continue to fluctuate between escalation and deescalation? There are three different ways to answer such questions: to look at the origins of conflict, to consider conflict actions, and to focus on conflict dynamics. This chapter considers the first problem, origins due to goal incompatibility.

Clearly, there are any number of specific reasons why two conflict actors can have incompatible goals. But it is possible to subsume them under three main headings: contested resources, incompatible roles, and incompatible values. This point is so important that it is worth representing it graphically (see Figure 3.1).

## Contested Resources

As the term suggests, resources are contested when a party wants some of the resources the other party has or when both adversaries want the same unallocated resource. Let us consider the main types of such resources, and then ask why a party may want more than it has already.

### Frequently Contested Resources

Humans can fight about a bewildering variety of things: about money, about land, about children, about infidelity, about politics. And yet

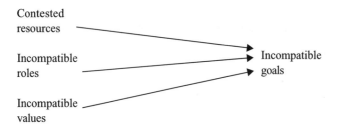

**Figure 3.1.** Possible Causes of Goal Incompatibility

it is possible to reduce this perplexing variety by classifying resources into three main categories: wealth, power, and prestige (Weber [1922] 1947).

*Wealth.* Because the first of the three main resources, wealth, usually involves "tangibles," it is easiest to understand. Today, when speaking of wealth, we tend to think of *money* – the source of much happiness and unhappiness, and of many conflicts. If you wish to see a conflict over money, attend a meeting at which the lawyer reads the last will of a recently deceased parent. The children, who in the past managed to get along in a reasonably civil manner will, more likely than not, be at each other's throats because each believes that he or she deserves more money than they actually got.

In ancient times the most important type of wealth was *land*, the source of prestige and power. Even though not as important as it once was, land is still a source of many serious conflicts. For example, both the Israelis and the Palestinians claim that East Jerusalem has historically been theirs and only they should have sovereignty there now. The Golan Heights, now occupied by the Israelis, was until 1967 a part of Syria and is claimed by it.

*Power.* There are those who seem to be bent on gaining and exercising power at all cost. They tell others what to do but respond angrily whenever others make suggestions to them; they monopolize conversations; they demand that they be treated with respect at all times. Nations can be – and usually are – equally power-hungry. They arm themselves to the teeth; they threaten their neighbors with armed intervention; they suppress internal dissention with force.

It is not difficult to identify actors who are powerful. But it is difficult to put your finger on what it is that they have. What exactly is power? While literature abounds with different definitions, we propose one that fits with our discussion of coerciveness: an actor is powerful if he or she can coerce others to do what he or she wants them to do *by altering their payoffs*: by either promising to reward the action he or she desires or by threatening to punish them if they fail to do so. Quite often, power is unequally distributed, with those who have only a little wanting more, those who have a lot wanting to keep it. Yet the very concept of "power inequality" is somewhat ambiguous, for it can have two quite different meanings.

First, power inequality may involve *domination*: party A has power over and dominates party B. Such situations often lead to a fight for liberation from oppression. Historical examples abound, ranging from slave revolts against Roman masters to the fight of Chechen rebels for independence from Russia. Second, power inequality exists when A does not dominate B, but has greater power *potential* than B does. This type of power inequality also can lead to conflict. This is because power is often a "zero-sum" commodity: if one party gains it, somebody else must lose it. Thus when the less powerful party seeks to increase its power potential, the more powerful party will resist these efforts.[1]

To illustrate the difference between these two types of power inequality, consider Germany following World War I. Through the Versailles treaty, Germany was reduced to a minor power and was required to pay heavy reparations to the victorious allies. This gave the allies power to dominate Germany's economy. When Hitler became the chancellor of Germany, he reduced this power by blatantly ignoring the Versailles treaty. In addition, by rearming Germany, he made that nation stronger, thus increasing its power potential. Just how much the balance of power had shifted toward Germany was shown when Hitler invaded Austria and Czechoslovakia with impunity. This would not have happened before Germany's rearmament.

*Prestige.* Street gang members constantly strive to gain a reputation for being tough and fearless, often by such acts as drive-by shootings. Often, there is conflict within a gang as young members try to show that they are tougher than their current leader. Gang leadership can change rapidly and often. Similarly, movie or rock stars are adored by their fans for only short periods of time, being soon displaced by new idols.

In these examples the struggle is about *prestige* (also referred to as "reputation," "respect," or "esteem"), the third most important contested resource. It is a scarce resource because, by definition, it presupposes ranking from the most respected to the least, and because most of us desire high prestige but only a few can have it at any given time.

Prestige is often closely linked with power: a person who has power is often held in high respect; a person who is highly respected often can acquire power. Yet prestige is conceptually different from power. Whereas power is based on the ability to alter another's payoffs, prestige is based on the ability to live up to the group's ideals. We respect, admire, and listen to an outstanding athlete, a saint, a successful general, a Nobel laureate.

Because prestige is earned by exemplifying a group's ideals, and because in modern societies different groups have different ideals, a person who enjoys high prestige in one group or one setting may have low prestige in another. This is due to the fact that membership in different groups is assigned different values. Thus, in the days of racial segregation, famous black entertainers such as trumpeter Louis "Satchmo" Armstrong might receive a standing ovation from their audiences and still not be allowed to dine or stay in the very clubs where they performed. At the same time, it is possible to gain respect from those who have denied it in the past, and to do so through conflict action. For example, denying African Americans seating in the front of the bus in the segregated South was a sign of disrespect. The civil rights struggle not only forced southern states to discontinue this practice, but also earned higher respect for blacks. This was finally accomplished when – and only when – it was made clear by civil rights activists and federal courts that such disrespect was contrary to the basic values of American society.

### Reasons for the Contest

Obviously, there are many reasons why one actor may want somebody else's resources. A playground bully may try to take away another child's toys because of his sociopathic personality; Japan may have embarked on its expansionist policies during World War II because it lacked natural resources such as oil. But perhaps the most common reason for a contest – and one that has been theorized about most – is injustice: one party has resources that rightfully belong to another party.

*Injustice.* Justice and injustice are among the most elusive and disputed concepts in social theory. And yet, without having a clear idea of what is and is not unjust, it would be nearly impossible to understand many conflicts. The concept of *distributive justice* yields one clear definition. Although this concept is quite old, its importance was recently re-emphasized by Walton and McKersie (1965). But for us, the clearest and most complete exposition is again by George Homans (1974).

Roughly speaking, Homans argues that most of us live by the same basic principles: we believe that we are treated unjustly if we receive less *reward* than is appropriate (proportional) to our *contribution* to the group and to our *investments* in the group.[2] For example, factory workers will compare the wages they are paid and the enjoyment they derive from their work (their rewards) with the hours they have to work, their level of responsibility, and the tension it generates (their contributions), and with their seniority, amount of education, and membership in prestigious groups (their investment).

If the distribution of wealth, prestige, and power is – and is believed to be – unjust, those treated unjustly will desire to get more than they are currently receiving.[3] This creates incompatible goals: the privileged wish to maintain the status quo, the underprivileged to change it to their advantage. But there are at least two reasons why the theory of distributive justice alone might not account adequately for what is viewed as fair and just.

One reason is that its principles can be at odds with a society's culture. In some cases, culture is so strong that it totally overrides the principles of distributive justice. For example, Egyptian pharaohs were believed to be gods who must be obeyed, right or wrong. In other cases, culture is weaker, and beliefs in distributive justice coexist with widely held cultural beliefs. For example, American culture emphasizes equality, usually equality of opportunity but sometimes even equality of results. Some hold that wealth, prestige, and power should be equally distributed: they view the very rich with suspicion, call bosses by their first names, and resent being told what to do, even by their bosses. And yet these Americans also abide by the principles of distributive justice: they believe that parents should have more power than their children, that a competent employee should be paid better than one who does not do her job properly, that a law-abiding person should be respected more than a criminal.

The second problem is that Homans's theory is often difficult to use in practice. The privileged are bound to argue that their contributions and investments are higher, just as surely as the underprivileged will argue that they are not. Thus less controversial criteria are needed, such as *relative deprivation* – a concept that plays a crucial role in the conflict theory developed by Gurr (1970).

If you are gainfully employed, you may decide that you are treated unfairly by comparing yourself to others who have jobs similar to yours. If you find that they are being rewarded more than you are, you feel "relatively deprived." Thus fire fighters will compare their salaries with those of police officers, police in one city will compare themselves with those in another, and so on.

True, for the reasons mentioned earlier, some clearly deprived groups do not make such comparisons. For example, in traditional Hindu society, the members of the outcaste groups did not compare themselves unfavorably to the members of the higher castes such as the Brahmins, even though they were much poorer and had to work very hard at menial jobs. This was because the Hindu religion taught that people's position in life was a reflection of their performance in their previous life: a person who had lived a good life would, in the next life, move into a higher caste; a person who failed to live meritoriously would move to a lower caste or out of the system completely. Thus the power, wealth, and prestige of the Brahmins were seen as rewards for their exemplary previous lives. By contrast, the outcastes were believed to deserve their lowly position because they had not behaved well in their previous lives. Consequently, the caste system was seen as just – although that belief weakened in the second half of the twentieth century.

Feelings of injustice can also occur when we compare what we get now to what we were getting in the past. Thus social conflicts tend to occur when economic depression creates wide-scale unemployment. Or we may compare what we are receiving to what we have been promised. In some cases, the promises are implicit. For example, in a broad historical perspective, popular uprisings seem to be more likely when the conditions of the oppressed are beginning to get better than when they remain at the same low level. This is because the improvements cause the oppressed to believe that they were "promised" more than any regime can deliver.[4]

One can put up with a lot if the demands made by others are sanctioned by the society itself: children tend to obey their parents, soldiers their officers, students their teachers. But if the legitimacy of the "rulers" is in doubt, rebellion rather than obedience may be forthcoming. Max Weber ([1922] 1947) discussed three conditions under which domination is likely to be viewed as *legitimate* and therefore just.

The first condition exists primarily in small tribal societies. In these groups, a leader is viewed as legitimate if he has charisma,[5] that is, if he can perform acts of exceptional bravery or miracles such as walking on water, healing the sick, or raising the dead. Although charisma is of crucial importance in tribal societies, it is also of some importance in modern societies. When a leader addressing a large audience is able to keep it spellbound, he or she has charisma. Orators such as Adolf Hitler or Martin Luther King and great actors such as Laurence Olivier had charisma. Mediocre speakers and actors do not.

Charismatically legitimated power is very unstable, because the leader who fails to perform extraordinary feats continuously will come to be seen as illegitimate. For this reason, charismatic power is often routinized into a second type, one that Weber calls "traditional." This type of power is found mostly in preindustrial societies that are fairly large and lead a settled life. As the name suggests, in these societies a ruler is viewed legitimate if he or she has acquired power and wields it in a manner prescribed by the customs of the community. For example, William the Conqueror, being an illegitimate son of an English king, was not selected as that king's successor, and had to take the throne by invading England.

In modern societies legitimate power tends to be of the third, or bureaucratic type.[6] A person holding a high position in a bureaucracy is presumed to have legitimate power if he or she was chosen in accordance with specific written rules and follows the prescriptions of the office. Thus Richard Nixon was forced to resign when he was widely seen as having violated the duties of the U.S. presidency.

*Absolute Deprivation.* While a sense of injustice may be the most important reason why one party wants more than it has, there are other reasons. One of these is "absolute" deprivation. It occurs when a party is deprived of whatever it needs to lead a decent life. For example, during the early 1800s, the relationship between the Apache tribes and the Spanish and Anglo settlers in northern Mexico and southeastern Arizona was relatively peaceful as long as the Spanish colonial government of Mexico provided the Apaches with regular rations of food.[7] But when the Mexican Revolution of 1810 drained government resources, those rations dwindled and became insufficient. In 1824 the Apaches bolted from their settlements and began raiding white settlements. A lengthy war between the settlers and the Indians ensued (Sweeney 1991).

*Belligerent Culture or Personality.* The word "belligerence" is derived from Latin for "waging war" (*Webster's* 1976, 102). Although today the term has several commonly accepted meanings, we shall use it here to mean a *disposition toward coercive action.*[8] Thus a wife may be always finding fault with what the husband does, one of a set of siblings may fight constantly, Germany may start many wars. When adversaries have incompatible goals, even when none of the obvious causes – such as injustice – is operating, the cause may be a belligerent personality or culture.

Often, we can gain considerable insight into a conflict if we know the actors' *culture.* For example, if we know that Apache men were expected to be warlike and the Hopi to be peaceful, we can understand why Apaches routinely raided other tribes. But if we wish to gain deeper theoretical understanding, we need to ask why these cultural differences exist in the first place. One of the most plausible explanations refers to the actors' "mode of production."

According to this theory, the Hopi, earning their living by agriculture, had to live settled lives and, thus provided with enough resources to live, developed little desire to attack others. Being dependent on having farming technology, they gradually developed a culture that valued hard work and was peaceful. The Apaches, on the other hand, relied primarily on hunting. Because they needed to move frequently to follow game, and even then often went hungry; because they often encountered opposition from other tribes; and because they had to use weapons when hunting or fighting, they developed a culture that valued bravery and was warlike.

The second main reason for inherent belligerence is the actors' *personality*. For example, a playground bully will always attack other children, taking away their toys; some football players will fight hard to score even when they have been injured. Once again, knowing the actor's personality helps us to understand why he or she is engaged in a conflict. But why do personalities differ?

One reason has just been discussed – the actor's culture. Parents bring up their children to uphold the values of their society; thus their personality is, to some extent, a reflection of that culture. Because the Hopi praised their children for cooperative behavior, the Hopi tended to be peaceful toward others; because the Apache rewarded their children for bravery and aggressiveness, Apache adults tended to be belligerent even toward each other.

But noncultural factors shape personality as well. Some aspects of personality – such as intelligence – seem to be genetically determined. But an actor may also become habitually belligerent if his or her aggressive behavior has been well rewarded in the past. For example, a boy who has been a successful athlete in high school may become a highly aggressive business executive.

Whatever its causes, belligerence contributes to goal incompatibility. Thus the playground bully may have the goal of taking away another child's toy, while that child will have the goal of keeping it; the Apaches who attacked a ranch often had the goal of taking away the rancher's cattle, while the rancher's goal was to keep his cattle for himself.

## Incompatible Roles

Two parties can have incompatible goals because they play different roles in an institution or an organization. The so-called functional school of theorizing explains role differentiation by noting that societies work better if they divide their labor.[9] Industrial societies have several social institutions, each attending to specific functions. They have families to provide a haven for family members and to raise children; religions to define and enforce main moral values; political institutions to set common goals and to distribute resources; economic institutions to produce goods and services (Parsons and Smelser 1956). Moreover, modern societies create organizations that further differentiate labor: management coordinates the work; engineers design the products; workers produce them; and salespeople sell them. Thus most employees play a role that has been assigned to them.[10]

### Vertical Differentiation

Sociologists have paid most attention to what might be called vertical role differentiation. It assigns different roles to different positions within the power hierarchy. This differentiation occurs within both social institutions and groups: parents have power over their children, ministers over their parishioners, managers over workers, government officials over citizens. Sociologists have long studied vertical role differentiation and the resulting conflict, especially in industrial organizations, but they have not always agreed on why the conflict exists. Karl Marx, who initiated inquiry into this problem, explained it in one way; Ralf Dahrendorf, another German sociologist, quite differently.

*Marx's Theory.* Marx developed a complex theory of social systems, one that was augmented and changed over the years. Yet there is a continuing theme in his writing that ties social conflict to private ownership: social conflicts exist because there are those who own the means of production and those who work for the owners (Marx and Engels [1846] 1947). The goals and interests of these two groups are incompatible, and they are therefore inevitably in conflict with each other.

What constitutes the "means of production" depends on the mode of production. In feudal societies the main mode of production was agriculture; hence the main means of production was land. Land pitted those who owned it, the aristocracy, against those who worked on it, the peasants, serfs, and slaves.[11] In capitalist societies, the main means of production is capital, most notably factories and information. The basic cleavage is between those who own the capital (the capitalists, also known as the bourgeoisie) and those who work for them (the proletariat).

Marx's analysis of conflict in capitalist societies led him to conclude that the capitalist's relentless pursuit of profit creates many problems for the workers. He argued that, in the long run, there is only one way a capitalist can make a profit – by exploiting workers. He must pay them less than the goods they produce are worth. In fact, Marx believed that capitalists will always try to reduce the wage to a mere subsistence level, to a point where it is barely sufficient for the survival of the worker and his family. Not surprisingly, the proletariat's goal is the opposite: to raise wages to a fair level.

Marx saw additional reasons for the incompatibility between bourgeoisie and proletariat in goals and interests. In their ruthless pursuit of profit, capitalists dehumanize their workers. They do not hesitate to tear them away from their families and their churches, to turn them into machines doing boring and repetitive work without knowing its purpose. Thus, the ultimate goal of the proletariat is (should be) the destruction of the capitalist system, just as the goal of the capitalist is the preservation of the system.

*Dahrendorf's Theory.* Subsequent writers found Marx's analysis wanting. Among the most influential is Ralf Dahrendorf (1959). Having criticized Marx's theory of conflict on the grounds that it has yielded predictions that proved false, he proceeded to make his most important point.[12] He argued that Marx failed to make correct predictions because he took into account only a special case of a more general phenomenon. Marx believed that private ownership of the means of production is the cause of social conflicts – that if it were eliminated, harmony would prevail. In point of fact, said Dahrendorf, the true cause is more general: it is an aspect of the vertical differentiation itself – the division between those who protect the interest of the whole, and the interests of the remaining group members.

The "whole versus part" aspect of vertical differentiation exists and creates incompatible goals in many diverse associations. In some cases, the incompatibility is between the stated goals of the organization and the goals of its members *as individuals.* For example, although priests and ministers should (and usually do) lead church members on the road to righteousness, some members find sinful ways more enjoyable. Although professors should (and often do) impart knowledge to students, some students wish to enjoy their stay at the university and study as little as possible. Although the commissioners of a county are responsible for collective needs such as well-kept roads and fire protection, some citizens are concerned only with lowering their taxes.

In other cases, the incompatibility is between the stated goals of the whole organization and the goals of those who are assigned more *specific tasks* within it. Thus the managers of a firm should see to it that the firm makes a good profit, while the engineers should design the best possible product, no matter how expensive it may be.

*Who Is Right?* To whom should you listen, to Marx, who often saw social conflict as rooted in private ownership, or to Dahrendorf, who attributed it to vertical role differentiation? As recent history has shown, this question is far from trivial. If you side with Marx, you may try to minimize social conflicts by eliminating private ownership – an approach adopted by Soviet leaders. If you listen to Dahrendorf, you may try to minimize concentration of power – an approach typical of Western democracies.[13]

We side with Dahrendorf, simply because his theory is more general and thus explains more than Marx's does. For example, why did the miners in the former Soviet Union rebel against their managers, even though the means of production were not privately owned? Why did the workers throw in their lot with the dissidents in communist countries such as Poland and Czechoslovakia? Dahrendorf's theory suggests that they rebelled because their interests and goals were different from those of the people who were responsible for the whole: the managers wanted to fulfill the current five-year plan, the workers wanted a decent living without backbreaking work.[14]

To get to the main thrust of our argument, we must make a technical point: although those who are responsible for the whole group nearly always have more power than those who are not, this book separates these two aspects of inequality. Earlier, we noted that those who have power tend to have different goals than those who do not; now we are saying that those who are responsible for the whole would have different goals than those who are responsible for the parts, *even if there were no power difference between them.*

This comparison puts Marx's theory in a new light. Marx was undoubtedly right when he spoke of the shameless exploitation of workers by nineteenth-century capitalists. However, one could point out – as would Dahrendorf – that this was not only because capitalists had unlimited power and used it to their own advantage, but also because they had to seek prosperity for the whole of their enterprises.

Thus the incompatibility of goals was due not only to exploitation by those with power, but also to the fact that capitalist enterprises had to make a profit in order to survive, while the workers had to have decent wages to live.

### Horizontal Differentiation

An organization or institution usually has role differentiation that is due to the very fact that many members have only partial and specific responsibilities. For example, an organization might have one type of role for engineers, another for salespeople, still another for accountants. Such role differentiation may be called horizontal to indicate that although the roles are different, the people playing them relate to each other as colleagues, not as superiors and subordinates.

On paper, the specialized roles are designed in such a way that they work in harmony to achieve a common purpose: the engineers prepare blueprints for the products, the salespeople endeavor to sell it, the accountants manage the finances. In reality, the goals assigned to different specialists may be incompatible. Suppose that an engineer is assigned the task of upgrading a jet fighter. She proceeds to do the best job she can, using the newest available technology. Often, this requires adding new equipment that, in turn, needs to be monitored by the pilot. Then the prototype of the redesigned fighter is given to a test pilot. He finds that the cockpit is so full of dials and levers as to be unmanageable. And the stage is set for a conflict: the engineers strive to include the newest technology; the test pilots want a plane that can be handled with ease.

## Incompatible Values

Groups that are separated from each other tend to develop different cultures that may advocate incompatible values – that is, the standards of rightness and goodness that hold a culture and society together. Let us consider how value incompatibility can happen.

### Separation

Any individual, separated from others, will in time develop a unique set of values. He or she will abandon these values in favor of group values only if he or she interacts frequently with the group members. The same is true for groups.

*Separation of Individuals.* Within-group interaction tends to be most intense in small tribal societies. Although a large society can preserve some of the features of a small group – Japanese society being a prominent example – in most instances large industrial societies tend to promote the culture of individualism, thereby inhibiting free within-group interaction. Individualism encourages the members to formulate and develop their own values rather than to accept those of their group. Just how extreme individualism can be is suggested by Bellah et al. (1986, 221): they found that, in the contemporary United States, some individuals had created a religion of their very own, with their own unique beliefs and rituals.

One of the reasons why individuals separated from others develop unique values is a difference in personalities: some are aggressive, others passive; some are talkative, others taciturn; some like to solve problems in solitude, others like to socialize. These personality differences can create value differences and lead to incompatible goals. Thus two roommates might be in conflict because one likes the room clean and well organized whereas the other likes to be free to put things wherever she wants. At times, these differences can erupt into conflict over seemingly trivial matters such as not keeping the cap on the toothpaste.

*Separation of Groups.* When a nomadic tribe moves into a new territory and becomes prosperous, its population grows in size. But a tribal society can function adequately only when it is small, say between fifteen and fifty members. When it grows larger, some of its members leave and create a new social unit at a new location. Given the physical separation, interaction between the original tribe and the new unit becomes minimal, while within each unit it is intense.[15] Ultimately, the two groups develop different cultures. For example, Swiss villages located in isolated valleys have developed unique dialects that are unintelligible to villagers in other valleys. Although such linguistic differences need not create incompatible values, sometimes they do. At the very least, each village considers itself superior to its neighbors.

Group separation has similar consequences in modern societies. Because members of separate groups seldom interact across their group's boundaries, their cultures become different – in some cases, incompatible. Consider, for example, the proliferation of cults in contemporary American society, ranging from religious cults that worship ancient gods to secular cults such as militias that oppose the government. Each group is small and has clearly defined beliefs, values, and norms that make it distinct from other cults and from mainstream culture.

*Personal and Group Identity.* An important reason why different actors have incompatible goals is that they – be they individuals or groups – value themselves much more highly than others value them. They feel that they are not fully appreciated by others, that they are not receiving their due: students are shattered if they receive a bad grade, employees feel almost invariably that they deserve higher pay, children feel that their siblings are loved more than they are. And, as has been observed by anthropologists, all societies are "ethnocentric," believing themselves better than others.

Not surprisingly, I need to justify why I am better than others think I am. So I construct an *identity* that proves it. I may believe that, although I did not have the same education as my colleagues, I have a better intuitive understanding of how to solve problems; that, although my parents were poor farmers, I am just as good as anybody else because I have an ancestor who came to America on the *Mayflower*; that, although my business is not doing very well, I have always treated my customers fairly. Similarly, groups develop identities that justify their imagined superiority: the French may believe that they are more cultured than the Americans; the southern whites that they are more industrious and honest than the blacks; the Apaches that they are braver than the Hopis.

A discussion of group identity would be incomplete without considering its current version, one that exists primarily in large contemporary societies. It occurred as a result of several developments happening more or less simultaneously, such as industrialization and urbanization, population growth and mobility, and technological advances – especially in communication and transportation. These changes made it possible to mobilize the population of large societies such as France and the United States, and unify it through a commonly held set of values – values that became known as *nationalism*: a desire to achieve, maintain, and perpetuate the identity, integrity, prosperity, and power of the entire nation (Christenson et al. 1975, 24–30).

Perhaps all groups in danger of losing their identity will fight. Chicanos wish to preserve their language and cultural heritage and resist attempts at assimilating them into Anglo culture. Even the friendliest Indian tribes have turned to warfare once the whites started to take away their land or despoil their sacred grounds. Ethnic groups within the Soviet Union declared their independence as soon as the power of the central government diminished. But nationalism, because it occurs in large societies equipped with modern and deadly weapons, changed the nature of conflict dramatically, making it so destructive as to threaten the very existence of humankind.

### Values of Communities and Systems

It is impossible to predict in detail what culture will be created by separated groups. Some tribes worship the sun, others the ocean; some societies prescribe that one should eat with forks and knives, others that one ought to use chopsticks. But in certain very general respects one can predict the type of values a society will develop: small tribal societies tend to develop "communal" values, whereas large industrial societies tend to adopt "system" values.

Classical sociologists, trying to explain the functioning of societies, found that they could not do so without distinguishing between two broad types of social arrangements. At first, they thought that this distinction was linked to historical development. They believed that early, preindustrial societies had social arrangements and values quite different from those of the emerging industrial societies. Although this point was made most forcefully by German sociologist Ferdinand Tönnies ([1887] 1963), other sociologists made similar observations. Because each of them arrived at this conclusion from a different starting point, they all conceptualized this variation somewhat differently and gave it different names.[16] But contemporary German sociologist Jürgen Habermas (1987) argues that all societies have both types of these arrangements, that they differ merely in how important each arrangement is. He calls these two types of arrangements "lifeworld" and "system." This book uses his term "system" but not – because it seems confusing to many – his term "lifeworld." Instead, we shall speak about "communities" and "communal" values.

American sociologist Talcott Parsons (Parsons and Shills 1951) developed a theory that helps us understand these differences. He noted that before specific social arrangements can be created, five basic decisions must be made. Should the relationships between members be affective or affectively neutral, self-oriented or collectively oriented, universalistic or particularistic, specific or diffuse, ascriptive or achievement-oriented?

These distinctions may be illustrated by contrasting the values of a mother with those of a surgeon. Whereas a mother is expected to relate to her children in an "affective" and loving way, a surgeon should never get emotionally involved with his or her patients and thus never treats members of his or her own family. Whereas a mother should have a "collectivist" orientation, caring for her children as much as or more than she cares about herself, a surgeon is expected to be strongly motivated by money and reputation. Whereas a mother should have a "particularistic" orientation toward her children, believing them to be the most beautiful and the smartest, a surgeon should provide the same quality of service universally, to all patients. Whereas a mother's role is defined in a "diffuse" manner – she is expected to be a nurse, a chauffeur, a teacher, or whatever is called for – a surgeon typically is a specialist, perhaps performing only heart surgeries. Finally, whereas a mother's role is defined in an "ascriptive" fashion – because only a woman can perform it and (until very recently) most women were expected to perform it – anybody who completes the requisite medical training achieves the status of a surgeon.

Once a society has specified its preferred types of relationships, it has created a social structure and, in effect, inaugurated a set of cultural values. Although any combination of values is possible, they often tend to coalesce into two mutually exclusive sets. One set is typical of communities, the other of industrial systems (see Table 3.1).

Different structures promote different types of values. Communal values are created spontaneously when members of a society engage in *free, face-to-face communication* that can occur only in small groups. Early in history, communal values were found in small tribes; today

Table 3.1. *Values of Communities and
Industrial Systems*

| Communal Values | Values of Industrial Systems |
|---|---|
| Be affective | Be affectively neutral |
| Be collectivistic | Be self-oriented |
| Be particularistic | Be universalistic |
| Be ascriptive | Be achievement-oriented |
| Be diffuse | Be specific |

they exist in small groups such as families, clubs, or religious cults. Although communal values originate in small groups, they can also be found in certain larger groupings that were derived from the original small groups: Christian Scientists, Alcoholics Anonymous, the National Organization for Women. And although their cultures may differ in many respects, they are similar in that they tend to adopt the values of the community.

The values of the "system" emerge when a society attempts to solve its problems in an *instrumentally rational* way,[17] especially when members of a society attempt to solve problems posed by their "environment." As Parsons has noted, when the members consider how best to "adapt" to the environment – how to organize themselves in order to extract raw materials and transform them into usable goods – they tend to create economic organizations and institutions. And in industrial societies, these organizations and institutions tend to be bureaucratic, that is, hierarchical, formal, and highly differentiated. Hence the industrial system has the values listed in the right column of Table 3.1.

Before leaving this topic, we must clarify one point. Whereas all communities promote the values listed in the first column of Table 3.1, only *industrial* systems promote the values listed in the right column. Other types of systems may promote some of the communal values. For example, the Catholic Church, which reflects many of the values of feudal systems, does not assign specialized roles to those at the lower levels of its hierarchy: a priest is expected to minister to all spiritual needs of his parishioners. Moreover, the church teaches the collectivistic values of self-sacrifice and emphasizes affective values such as "love thy neighbor." The systems of future societies may also be expected to advocate many of the communal values.[18]

Habermas (1987) has pointed out that the difference between communal and system values can be a source of social conflict. In fact, he argued that in the advanced industrial societies the system "colonizes" and "deforms" communal life. For example, money and power interfere with the free interaction that is at the heart of communities (Ritzer 1992, 446).

### Role Differentiation

Role differentiation tends to create incompatible goals directly, by asking those who play different roles to act in incompatible ways. But it can also create incompatibility indirectly, by promoting different values. Teachers and educators not only have the goal of teaching their students, they also tend to value knowledge as such. Military officers not only have the goal of creating units that will fight well but also cherish the values of honor and obedience. And so on.

Some roles emphasize communal values; others, system values. For example, a minister is likely to emphasize the need for universal love, one of the primary communal values. A businessman, on the other hand, is just as likely to feel that in the business context efficiency – a value of the industrial system – is more important than active concern for others.

## Conclusions

We began by explaining goal incompatibility in terms of three main causes: contested resources, incompatible roles, and incompatible values. We can now elaborate on that explanation. Although the more detailed explanation, shown in Figure 3.2, is too complex to be quickly understood, you can profit from it if you are willing to spend some time studying it: you will come to understand how the causes depicted in the simpler graph of Figure 3.1 are themselves produced.

Figure 3.2 shows that there are three main reasons why you might *contest the distribution of resources*: because you believe that you are treated unjustly, because you do not have enough to live decently ("absolute" deprivation), or because you have a belligerent culture

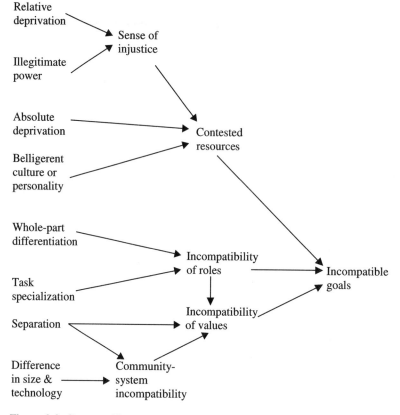

**Figure 3.2.** Causes of Incompatible Goals

or personality. It further shows how you can document injustice: by showing that you are deprived in comparison to others, or by proving that those who have power hold it illegitimately.

The graph also reminds us that *role incompatibility* exists for one of two main reasons: either because "vertical" differentiation assigns those in power the responsibility for the whole organization while assigning to the remaining members only specialized tasks; or because "horizontal" differentiation assigns specialized tasks to different members.

Finally, Figure 3.2 shows that there are three general reasons why two parties may have *different values*: because they play different roles, because they have been separated from each other, and because their groups differ in size and technology. Differences in size and technology matter because, when members of one party live in a small rural community while most of their opponents live in large industrial cities, the first party will have the "communal" values described in the first column of Table 3.1, the opponent the "system" values shown in the second column.

Figure 3.2 shows causes that may but need not operate in any specific conflict. The discussion of the next chapter makes this point vividly by showing that the U.S. civil rights conflict has only one main cause, while an organizational conflict to be discussed in Chapter 6 was shaped by several causes.

# CHAPTER FOUR

# Application to the Civil Rights Struggle

EVEN WHEN one has a general understanding of why conflicts occur, one may wish to know why a *specific* conflict has occurred. This chapter addresses that concern by applying the theory of the preceding chapter to the civil rights struggle in the United States.

## The African American Struggle for Equality

The most common type of internal conflict develops out of unjust inequality.[1] It is often manifested as the domination of one economic, cultural, or racial group by another. Such dominance produces the potential for conflict of such magnitude that it literally tears a society apart.

Most Americans would agree that the struggle between African Americans and American whites has been largely due to the unfair treatment of blacks, first as slaves, then as second- or third-class citizens. The blacks' goal of equality has been incompatible with the goal of continued dominance by whites. As obvious as that explanation might seem in the light of history, in this book we take nothing for granted, not even a universally held belief. We shall use our theory and known facts to determine whether this belief is correct. Most of the facts of the case can be summarized in a brief history of that struggle.

Before the Civil War, most African Americans were held in slavery. In the South their legal enslavement was soon thereafter replaced by

Jim Crow segregation, from which they then struggled to escape for nearly a century. In the southern United States, political and economic rights were still denied blacks well into the 1960s.

We should understand civil rights activism in the United States as a long historical progression with roots deep in pre-1950s history and branches in the form of other social movements its example has subsequently inspired. In the nineteenth century, of course, the abolitionist movement, slave rebellions, and the flight of slaves to freedom were all illustrations of resistance to racial injustice. Resistance from the pens and lips of Frederick Douglass, W. E. B. Dubois, Ida Wells, and many other black intellectuals had kept the flame alive through the turn of the century.

By the first decade of the twentieth century, African Americans were challenging racism with law as well as word. The National Association for the Advancement of Colored People (NAACP) was attacking racial segregation through the court system, an effort capped with enormous success in 1954 as the U.S. Supreme Court began dismantling legal segregation.

World War II provided an opportunity for the wedge of black organized labor to force open the world of better work and pay. A. Philip Randolph, head of the sleeping car porters union, had secured from a reluctant President Roosevelt assurance of equal access for blacks to work in the defense industries. That reluctance was overcome only with huge street marches and Randolph's credible threat of a mass disruption by blacks if they were shut out. One might say that this action was the first event in the mass direct action of the civil rights movement. The wider labor movement then began recruiting the increasing number of African Americans who subsequently joined the industrial ranks during the war.

With the end of the war, racial discrimination throughout the United States was challenged by black veterans returning to a society unwilling to reward them justly for their military service. A substantial black middle class, bred within an energized black religious movement, was emerging to lead a broad-based challenge to discriminatory inequality (Frazier 1962). A deepening sense of injustice was shaping a monumental grievance among blacks and sympathetic whites, a grievance soon to be transformed into overt conflict action in what is commonly known as the civil rights movement.

From the 1950s onward, civil rights protest and action took various forms: litigation such as the action that produced the 1954 Supreme Court decision outlawing racial segregation; direct intervention such as sit-ins; self-help programs like Jesse Jackson's Operation PUSH, Freedom Summer, the Mississippi Democratic Freedom Party, and the Black Panther Party; and federal affirmative action.

This mobilization to mass action of blacks that clarified goal incompatibility between white and black America was made possible through greater access of blacks to necessary resources for that mobilization – educated leaders, money, a growing social infrastructure in their communities. But it was also greatly facilitated by the changing post–World War II political opportunity structure (McAdam 1982), a new openness even in the upper South that would permit such a vital movement to develop.

The conflict over civil rights prepared the way for other conflicts over unjust inequality. One group of sociologists, theorists of new social movements, gives the civil rights movement much of the credit for many of the other change movements that followed it (Melucci 1980). Student power, women's rights, the Greens, liberation theologists all drew confidence, strategy, and tactics from civil rights protest. In the United States, the influence of civil rights is particularly striking. If we "fast-forward" the story by thirty years, we find numerous underrepresented groups working to equalize access to the U.S. system of opportunity and rewards. In universities and corporations, for example, especially at upper levels of power and privilege, we find those groups up against a "glass ceiling" of discriminatory treatment in promotion and rewards policies. That such racial, ethnic, and gender discrimination is real, not simply perceived, is verified in periodic investigative reports and successful court challenges. A prominent case in point is the 1996 "Jelly Bean" episode, in which Texaco executives were quite literally "taped in the act" of making racially discriminatory policy (*New York Times*, November 4, 1996). In that case, leaders in the African American community have responded in two directions: economic action in the form of a national boycott of Texaco products; legal action through a suit against Texaco for its violation of civil rights laws.

Perception of unjust inequality as a conflict source is not limited, however, to underrepresented or minority individuals and groups.

Affirmative action programs, implemented to eliminate discrimination and remedy past inequity, have created some strange bedfellows: whites who perceive "reverse discrimination" where so-called protected classes are given preference in hiring and economic assistance, all other criteria being equal; and some minority members, who argue that affirmative action undermines the credibility of the achievements of minority people "making it on their own." Such laws as California's Proposition 209 prohibiting government affirmative action illustrate the complex practical outcomes of presumably unjust inequality.

Although the direct action phase of the civil rights movement is for the most part history, that action built a strong base for a movement that is alive and well today. One has only to note the immediate and vigorous response by civil rights organizations and leaders such as Jesse Jackson to alleged disenfranchisement of tens of thousands of African American voters in Florida in the 2000 presidential elections. Movement caretaker organizations (Morris, 1984) such as the NAACP have demonstrated unusual vigor around that issue. This sensitivity of southern blacks to voting rights assurance has its taproot in the voting rights phase of the movement that was particularly costly for the black and white activists in the early 1960s who fought and occasionally died for the right to vote (McAdam 1988).

## Worldwide Influence of the Struggle

The American civil rights movement illustrates more than the development of incompatible goals as a stage in the growth of conflict. It also exemplifies the substantial influence social movements can have on one another – stimulating action, sharing ideas, modeling approaches for challenging sociopolitical structures. For example, the leaders, techniques, successes, and failures of American civil rights activism have had a sizable effect on the thought and action of the South African liberation movement to end apartheid.

Martin Luther King Jr.'s use of disciplined nonviolence was a clear stimulator of black South Africans' initial use of mass noncooperation with racial segregation in 1957 with the Johannesburg-Pretoria bus boycott. Begun spontaneously on January 7, 1957, their boycott followed a similar year-long effort by blacks in Montgomery, Alabama, which ended successfully in December 1956 (Karis and Gerhart 1977, 275).

As in the American movement, this successful challenge through refusing economic cooperation with a hated system galvanized the spirit of resistance. "South Africa was filled with a new excitement, and there was ample evidence, in the boycott and elsewhere, that resistance was beginning to assume a mass character," observed Chief Albert Luthuli (Luthuli 1962).

In fact, were we to trace this technique of mass noncooperation back to Gandhi, we would find his first use of disciplined nonviolent refusal to cooperate with an oppressive state occurring in South Africa itself. It then returned with him to India, migrating thereafter to King's southern United States and coming full circle to Mandela's South Africa.

Just as the early enthusiasm and multiracial solidarity of the U.S. movement gave way in the mid-1960s to black separatism (Wehr 1968), so too did South African resistance. The impact of American black power on the South African black consciousness movement was striking, both politically and culturally.

The literature of black American activism reached South Africa through bookstores and libraries, and some made its way directly into black student networks through white liberals sympathetic to the emerging spirit of black militancy. Most avidly consumed were *Soul on Ice* by Eldridge Cleaver, *Black Power: The Politics of Liberation in America* by Stokely Carmichael and Charles Hamilton, and the *Autobiography of Malcolm X*. Tapes of speeches delivered by Malcolm X and Martin Luther King also circulated among students. American catchwords like "relevance" and "power structure" entered South African political discourse, along with the term "black consciousness" itself, and the aggressive visual symbol of the upraised fist (Karis and Gerhart 1997, 105–106).

Black consciousness ideologist Steven Biko proclaimed in 1967 that black South Africans "must build themselves into a position of non-dependence upon whites" (Woods 1987, 39), thereby anticipating the steadfast self-reliance that was ultimately to permit a negotiated end to apartheid in the 1990s.

Just as black militancy and separatism were probably necessary for survival and success of the American racial justice effort, so too might South African racial liberation have failed without it. The use of disciplined nonviolence and its eclipse by strident militancy were not the only evidence of the American movement's influence on South African activism. The role of the black church leaders and university students as organizers and ideologues of the movement were also mirrored in the South African experience.

The influence of American civil rights activism on South African liberation teaches us a powerful lesson. Social movements continue far beyond their immediate time and place. Their experience is shared within and beyond the societies in which they develop. They borrow from other movements and lend to yet others. This appears ever more the case as communication accelerates and proliferates in the electronic world.

## Theoretical Analysis

This history gives a fairly complete picture of the civil rights struggle: how it started, how it intensified, where it stands today, and how it influenced movements in other countries. Yet, paradoxically, this gives us more facts than we need at this point, because our objective in this chapter is limited to identifying the "root causes" of the civil rights struggle – the causes of incompatibility between the goals of the African Americans and those of the white establishment. This means that we do not consider, at this point, how resources were mobilized and employed or how the conflict escalated and deescalated through its history. We could offer a full explanation only at the end of this book, only after we have considered why hidden conflicts become overt (Chapter 5) and why conflicts escalate and deescalate (Chapter 7).

Even though our objective in this chapter is limited to explaining why African Americans and traditional southern whites tend to have incompatible goals, we can proceed best if we begin by outlining general guidelines for applying our theory to a specific conflict.

### *General Procedure*

It has been said that a picture is worth a thousand words. Believing that this is true, we start by presenting our theory in graphic form, as in Figure 3.2. We then proceed systematically to ask questions suggested by that figure. As we are interested in *explaining* the conflict, we move from right to left in the diagrams. If we were interested in *predicting* whether two individuals or groups will develop incompatible goals, or if we were interested in minimizing the incompatibility, we would move in the opposite direction.[2]

Our first question focuses on the variable at the extreme right: What evidence is there that the two parties (blacks and whites) had incompatible goals? If the parties are shown to have such goals, our next question searches for the direct causes of incompatibility,[3] such as, Did the parties have incompatible goals because one of them contested the distribution of resources? If they did, we ask questions such as, Was the distribution of resources questioned because it was felt to be unjust? If we find that to be the case, we probe even further by asking, for example, Was the sense of injustice due to relative deprivation? And so forth.

Before this procedure is illustrated on the civil rights movement, it ought to be added that its application is never routine. Rarely do historical facts yield uncontestable evidence. This means that different investigators might come up with somewhat different explanations, even if they all were using the same procedure. It also means that finding reasons for incompatibility can be quite challenging and creative. Still, why don't you consider the ensuing analysis, always feeling free to come to different conclusions than we do?

### Are the Goals Incompatible?

You may find – as we did – that the most compelling evidence for goal incompatibility is the fact that the civil rights struggle has been going on for a considerable period of time. For at least a half century now, African Americans have been trying to coerce the dominant white majority to accept the goal of racial equality, using litigation, demonstrations such as sit-ins, and, most recently, enforcement of affirmative action and voting rights protection. And southern whites have responded by actions ranging from mob violence to police attacks on civil rights protesters and, most recently, to discriminatory hiring and promotion practices.

At this point you may remember something that casts doubts on this conclusion. Have we not argued, in Chapter 2, that conflicts can be driven not only by incompatible goals but also by hostility? Is it, therefore, not possible that the conflict has lasted this long because of the enduring hostility between the two sides, rather than because of their goal incompatibility? True enough – the duration of the conflict is, at best, only circumstantial evidence, one that by itself cannot establish that incompatible goals exist. We thus may have to shift our attention to the possible main *causes* of goal incompatibility: contested resources, incompatibility of roles, and incompatibility of values (see Figure 3.2). Are any of these causes operative?

### Are Resources Contested?

What evidence is there that the civil rights struggle has been about the distribution of scarce resources, notably wealth, power, and prestige? Consider the following: voter registration activities by blacks have greatly increased their political power; their work for affirmative action is aimed at making them wealthier and more powerful; their protest activities such as sit-ins are undertaken to increase their prestige. Many dominant whites have opposed these efforts, wanting things to remain as they were. Actions designed to prevent African Americans from achieving their goals have ranged from open intimidation to subtle discrimination in hiring and promoting practices.

Having concluded that African Americans did contest the distribution of resources, consider why they have contested them. Figure 3.2 suggests three possible reasons: because African Americans were treated unjustly by whites and resented it; because they were deprived "absolutely"; or because they and/or their white opponents were exceptionally belligerent. Which of these explanations applies?

*Injustice.* The literature makes it clear that African Americans have been deprived relative to other groups in American society. Evidence of that deprivation was presented by African American scholars like W. E. B. Dubois as early as 1899. A somewhat more recent – and widely accepted – study was done during the 1930s by Swedish economist Gunnar Myrdal (1944). His assessment of the relative deprivation of blacks in the United States, made with the critical, objective eye of a foreign observer, revealed to white America what black people knew well from their daily experience: "When, in this way, the data on the American Negro problem are marshaled under the high ideals of the American Creed, the fact must be faced that the result is rather dark. Indeed, the Negro Problem in America represents a moral lag in the development of the nation and a study of it must record nearly everything which is bad and wrong in America" (Myrdal 1944, ix).

Having prepared the reader for a very critical report, Myrdal proceeds to present (p. 365) empirical data supporting the claim that African Americans were suffering greatly at the hands of white America. One revealing figure the study presents is a wide family income disparity ($980 [black] vs. $1930 [white]) in New York in 1935, and a yet more striking ($576 vs. $1,876) differential in Columbia, South Carolina, in the same year.

At this point you may conclude – as we did – that these facts suggest that African Americans were deprived *relatively*. This conclusion is bolstered by the fact that, by the early 1950s, this became an officially recognized fact. The most striking evidence of that is the 1954 U.S. Supreme Court decision in *Brown v. Board of Education*, declaring public school segregation by race unconstitutional. This decision established that separate but equal facilities, even if they existed (which they nowhere did), would not suffice: that forced segregation in and of itself implied inequality and was therefore discriminatory. By the 1950s, the relative deprivation of African Americans could be clearly seen as a source of their deep sense of injustice and resentment.

Some black leaders – Marcus Garvey, Paul Robeson, Malcolm X – questioned the legitimacy of the U.S. political system, but, because there is no compelling evidence to suggest that most African Americans believe the U.S. government to be illegitimate (illegitimacy being the other possible cause of a sense of injustice), you may conclude that the main reason why American blacks feel that they are treated unfairly is their deprivation relative to the whites.

*Absolute Deprivation.* Figure 3.2 suggests that you should now ask, Have African Americans been deprived "absolutely," that is, did they, as a group, lack the minimal resources necessary for a decent life? If you were to search for relevant evidence, you would find that in 1976 the percentage of "officially poor" (those with income of less than $5,815) was 31 percent for black Americans but only 9 percent for white Americans (Light and Keller 1979, 270–271) and that in 1980 the percentage of unemployed was 19 percent for blacks but only 6 percent for whites (Manis 1984, 273). Moreover, you would find that some measures of poverty were increasing in the 1970s and 1980s. For example, the "lowest income" census tracts were populated mostly by African Americans – and not only has the number of poverty tracts more than doubled since 1970, but also the number of African Americans living in them grew by more than one-third from 1970 to 1990 (Wilson 1996, 15).

Thus you would probably conclude that African Americans have contested the distribution of valuable resources (wealth, power, and prestige) not only because they have been deprived relative to the whites, but also because many have been living in abject poverty – because they have been deprived absolutely.

*Belligerence.* Remembering that we defined belligerence as a "disposition toward coercive action" (see Chapter 3), can we say that the civil rights struggle was fueled by it? It would be hard to argue that the most prominent black leaders had belligerent *personalities.* After all, Dr. Martin Luther King Jr. preached nonviolent action; and his teachings were largely followed by the black community. But has African American *culture* been belligerent?

Studies suggest that groups that have been subjugated for a long period of time develop a culture that equips them to deal with oppression. Quite often, they learn how to appear obedient when odds are against them, and their lives are tolerable. They also learn to rebel when conditions become intolerable and the odds change in their favor. The history of slave revolts suggests that early black culture in the United States might have developed such a mixture of passivity and belligerence.

Black anger toward white society, however, became more visible with time. Even early on, during black enslavement, there were expressions of hostile feelings in the writings of free blacks. In the first half of the twentieth century, blacks organized quietly to show their anger. In the second half of that century, African American resentment was expressed more publicly. In 1956 Dr. Martin Luther King Jr. confronted racial injustice through nonviolent direct action. Within a few months, the Montgomery Bus Boycott had transformed King from a scholarly Baptist minister fresh from graduate school into a movement leader. Thousands of black students soon followed him in applying the principles and methods of noncooperation with evil in public places throughout the South.[4]

Despite the gains achieved by the civil rights movement, resentment continued among the black working poor and those approaching middle-class status who, regardless of their energetic pursuit of "the good life," saw themselves slipping behind. Even today, those African Americans who have "arrived" to live the American Dream of prosperity and high status experience "genteel" racism every time an empty taxicab ignores their hail or a white person crosses the street to avoid them. There continues, then, among American blacks a reason to be constantly ready to challenge behavior seen as discriminatory and unjust.

Does this mean, then, that black culture has become belligerent? Note that black groups that have advocated violence never gained wide popular support, and that violent crime in black neighborhoods seems mostly due to poverty, poor policing, and drug deals gone bad. Thus we conclude that while black culture began to favor a more active opposition to discrimination, it has not become belligerent.

### Are Roles Incompatible?

As Figure 3.2 shows, the next possibility is that conflict stems from a difference in roles. For this to be a cause, however, you must be dealing with a conflict within a single institution or organization. And because the civil rights conflict has been of national scope, the only organization that so qualifies is the U.S. government.[5] You thus must ask whether, within the U.S. government, African Americans were playing different roles than whites, and whether each group's pursuit of goals consistent with the roles of its members produced incompatibility.

Let us begin by considering the first possibility, *vertical* role differentiation. Within the U.S. government, did one racial group occupy positions that were responsible for the well-being of all citizens while the other occupied positions that were assigned only specific tasks or dealt with only some citizens? It is certainly the case that whites had (and still have) most of the executive positions within the federal government. But were the two groups fighting for what was consistent with their roles, the whites defending the interests of the whole society while the blacks were fighting only for their own interests? Some might argue that this was – and is – indeed happening. For example, the white-dominated government passes laws that presumably benefit the entire society, such as those against drug trafficking, but blacks have argued that these laws discriminate against them, because crack cocaine, which is more prevalent in the black community, was targeted in the legislation more than powder cocaine, which is used more frequently by affluent whites. African Americans could argue that whites are *not* defending the interests of the whole society but only their own wealth, power, and prestige. Thus, although we saw that power inequality was an important reason for goal incompatibility, we now conclude that the whole-part aspect of vertical differentiation is not.

The second possible cause of incompatibility is *horizontal* role differentiation, that is, the possibility that the two races play different but equal roles in the government. This would be the case if, for example, whites were predominantly employed in the federal justice system while blacks were employed primarily in the commerce and interior departments. This is clearly not the case, and we can thus eliminate horizontal role differentiation as a source of the conflict.

### Are Values Incompatible?

As is usual for subjugated people, during slavery black culture valued overt docility and covert rebelliousness. But when the American Declaration of Independence asserted that all men are created equal, when the abolitionist movement was started, when slavery was abolished, and when black authors began to emphasize resistance to racial injustice, black culture began to change. It began to value overt resistance to discrimination, and it became generally accepted that African Americans were entitled to the same opportunities for wealth, prestige, and power as were whites.

At the same time, the culture of most southern whites continued to reflect the values of the old feudal society. Its elitist and racist beliefs held that blacks, being inherently inferior to whites, were incapable of doing anything better than menial work. Thus their values were incompatible with those of the blacks, which led to incompatible goals: while most African Americans began to strive for equality, many whites throughout the United States – and particularly in the South – wished to preserve their privileged positions.

## Conclusions

Let us consider how you might represent this analysis graphically. You might begin by laying down a few reasonable rules:

1. Start by duplicating the graph that represents the relevant theory. In this case, this means duplicating the graph of Figure 3.2.
2. Eliminate from that diagram all the arrows that correspond to causes you found *not* to be important. For example, because we (and, presumably, you as well) concluded that lack of legitimacy was not an *important* factor, we eliminate the arrow linking "illegitimate power" with "sense of injustice."
3. Retain all the arrows originating in the causes you found operative.
4. Add any causes or terms that might improve your insight into the conflict. The history of the civil rights struggle suggests adding several causes, such as slavery, segregation, and discrimination.

Figure 4.1 represents the resulting explanation of the civil rights movement. As we noted earlier, this diagram does not explain *all* aspects of the movement – our theory is not as yet ready to do that. Still, it explains the "roots" of the struggle or, as we prefer to say, the reasons for goal incompatibility.

The figure shows that the goals of the blacks and whites have indeed become incompatible: most blacks wish to achieve equality, whereas many whites strive to preserve their privileges. It also shows that this incompatibility is due primarily to injustice, past and present (slavery, segregation, and discrimination) and to an incompatibility between emerging black culture (that emphasizes equality) and old southern white culture (that believes in white supremacy). The fact that there are no arrows originating in some variables, such as role incompatibility, indicates that some potential causes have not exercised important influence on the goals of the parties.

When viewing Figure 4.1, you should keep in mind two stipulations. First, you should recognize that the causes we omitted might exercise some influence, but if so, their influence is minor. Second, to apply our

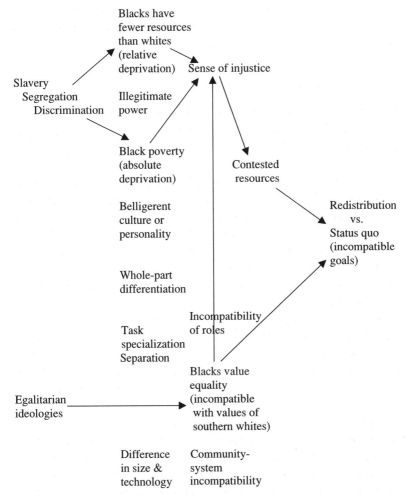

**Figure 4.1.** Main Causes of Goal Incompatibility in the Civil Rights Conflict

procedure, we often had to rely on our insights and go beyond the available facts. Thus you might interpret the same facts in a slightly different way and might come to a slightly different conclusion than we have.

## Letting Theory Inform Action

Perhaps this application of our theory will help you to see that our approach can be useful to observers and conflict actors alike – that knowing the underlying causes can help them make wiser, more effective conflict action choices. Some additional principles, based on practical experience, can be helpful.

### Some Practical Principles

After the participants in a specific conflict have applied our procedure and found what its main causes are, they should design strategies and tactics for dealing with it.

*Formulating a Strategy.* They may begin by addressing the basic causes of incompatibility. As Figure 4.1 suggests, the civil rights conflict could be minimized by reducing the relative as well as the absolute deprivation of African Americans. In fact, this has been attempted through the creation of programs and organizations such as the Community Relations Division in the U.S. Department of Justice, affirmative action, the U.S. Equal Employment Commission, and the U.S. Civil Rights Commission.

Next, the adversaries should set realistic goals that are based on their assessment of genuine incompatibilities present in the conflict. Each party in conflict generally has a preferred future – pleasant life conditions, reasonable relationships, having their basic needs met. African Americans in the 1960s, for example, wanted at least a desegregated society with equal rights, if an integrated one was not attainable. To engage in conflict one should carefully sketch out one's preferred future near the outset of conflict. That future may change somewhat during the conflict, but one should begin with a reasonably clear image of it. In the process of imaging that preferred future, a conflict party may discover that its goals are not as incompatible with those of its opponents as it earlier believed. Of course, it may also discover the opposite.

For some purposes, it is important to distinguish between interests and values. We saw in Chapter 2 that, in a payoff matrix, *interests* of an actor are all the outcomes that have positive payoffs for him or her. In practice, one often focuses on interests that are shaped by more or less universal needs such as food, shelter, safety from attack, and so forth. *Values*, on the other hand, are the general standards of goodness, rightness, and preference that the actor believes in – and they help to determine the specific payoffs within the payoff matrix. The adversaries' interests and values shape their preferred futures, which in turn shape their immediate goals.

Interests can be clarified internally, by each conflict party acting on its own. There is much to be said, however, for clarifying interests cooperatively with the other side. Being clear about your own interests in a conflict is usually helped by having your opponents clarify theirs as well. It is important to be clear about what it is you want your opponents to do that would bring about your preferred future. What must they do and how can you make it more likely that they will do it?

It usually is easier for us to know what the opponents want than *why* they want it, because their values are less visible than their specific goals. We have to hunt harder for them. Yet values are at the core of many conflicts. We must be aware of them before we can clarify the preferred future we ask our opponent to help us create.

Once conflict actors have clarified goal incompatibility, interests, and values, they should look for additional theories on which to base action. In some cases, they should look for new conceptual distinctions. For example, in "realistic" conflicts (where goal incompatibility is the major source of conflict), they may separate the opponents' primary goals (such as fair hiring practices) from their secondary goals (such as protecting a public "position" they may have taken). This distinction might lead to a "clarify interests, soften positions" strategy (Fisher and Ury 1981). If, on the other hand, the conflict is "nonrealistic" (i.e., is driven primarily by hostility), strategies may aim at reducing hostility – by validating the parties' feelings or allowing expressions of antagonism in caucus meetings from which the opponent is absent. Mediators often use such approaches to resolve community disputes that involve racial tensions.

Of paramount interest to any conflict party is to have its opponent do what it asks. One way you can facilitate that is to create a list of propositions acceptable to the opponent. You can begin, for example, with a simple chart of the likely positive and negative consequences for your opponent of doing and not doing what you ask. Then, you can imagine ways to increase the pluses in the "if they do" column and reduce those in the "if they don't" column. Roger Fisher applied this "acceptable proposition" technique as a consultant to the Carter administration in the Egyptian-Israeli Camp David negotiation.

The parties were persuaded to recast proposals into an acceptable form, permitting them to abandon their initial, ironclad, and non-negotiable positions. For example, a key provision in the final accord was the demilitarization of the Sinai Peninsula, something to which both sides had often publicly sworn they would not agree.

As you saw in Chapter 2, one possibility is to use persuasion, by drawing attention to some new aspects of the conflict. Sometimes refocusing may involve moving from ultimate goals to intermediate ones; at other times, it may require merely changing the time frame. For example, the shift from "immediately" to "at some undetermined future time" appeared sufficient to permit the Unionists in Northern Ireland to say yes to the Good Friday Agreement of 1998.

You can also increase the acceptability of a proposition by improving what will happen to the opponents if they agree. What are some improvements of higher value to them and lower cost to us that we could promise? You could also make your request as legitimate as possible, rooting it in universal standards of justice, fairness, and reason.

All parties in conflict have a preferred outcome or future. Too often, though, the fog of contention obscures those futures and why we want them. By mapping or assessing the values of the opposing sides (Wehr and Rohrbaugh 1978), we can better devise ways to resolve the conflict cooperatively. Once value preferences (justice, beauty, decent quality of life) begin to appear, it becomes clear how the preferences of opponents in a particular conflict overlap. The process often reveals much common ground. Also, once revealed, values clarify interests, in turn permitting opposing sides to craft propositions acceptable to one another.

A relevant technique was developed to help resolve a conflict over a proposed ski area in western Colorado. Residents of the county involved were deeply divided over the proposal. The decision was squarely before the county commissioners, with no referendum possible and only soundings from polarized interest groups on either side to guide their decision. A survey was then done of a random sample of county residents, who were asked to create their preferred future for the county, choosing differing amounts of several community values (e.g., open space, educational quality, pace of life, economic vitality). These value preferences (payoffs) were then averaged into a preferred future for county residents. That preferred future was then compared with predictions from impact assessment studies to give a rough measure of how closely the predicted changes from ski development would approximate the citizens' preferences. In that particular case, values mapping was used by a third party with the decisional responsibility for public policy. But there is no reason why the same technique could not also facilitate cooperative resolution in interpersonal and intergroup conflict.

### The Technique of Conflict Mapping

As conflict emerges, it produces considerable confusion. Interaction of the conflict parties changes, sometimes radically and abruptly. Levels of unpredictability, uncertainty, and emotion rise. Unwise and costly decisions are often made out of lack of understanding of what is occurring. Because how a conflict emerges largely determines how costly it will subsequently be, those involved should have the clearest possible understanding of what is going on as it emerges.

Even the simplest interpersonal conflict has many elements; a conflict that involves multiple parties, large numbers of people, and complex organizations can become enormously complicated. To understand it, you need both a general analysis, such as the kind presented in this book, and a more detailed, microanalytical approach, such as that of Deutsch (1973). The concept of "conflict mapping" helps one to clarify the conflict-generated confusion (Wehr 1979).

Every conflict has certain basic elements permitting you to produce a road map by which a conflict opponent, a third-party intervenor, or simply a student of conflict can find his or her way through it. Several steps are involved.

*Specify the Context.* The mapper first gathers information about the history of the conflict and its physical and organizational settings. Conflict does not emerge in a vacuum. Sometimes one conflict is nested within another. For example, a family conflict about finances may be a part of a wider conflict: how the children should be raised, how one should spend free time, who should make the major decisions.

*Identify the Parties.* Parties in a conflict differ in how directly they are involved and the importance of its outcome for them. Primary parties are those which oppose one another, are using coercive behavior, and have a direct stake in the outcome of the conflict. Secondary parties have an indirect stake in the outcome. They are often allies of the primary parties but are not direct adversaries. Third parties are actors such as mediators and peace-keeping forces that might intervene to facilitate resolution.

*Separate Causes from Consequences.* Distinguishing a cause of a conflict from its consequence is not always easy. In fact, as a conflict emerges, cause and consequence tend to blend. Hostility might be a consequence of one phase of a conflict and a cause of the next.

As you saw earlier, incompatibility of perceived goals and interests is perhaps the most basic cause of social conflict. Defense of one's identity often leads to such incompatibility, particularly in the contemporary world, where group awareness and rights have assumed high visibility. Cultural differences are sources of separateness and difference, and create a sense of self. Contrasting beliefs and values are operating vigorously in much social conflict. They range from a negative image of the opponent to an opinion about a supreme being.

Disagreement over facts characterizes much conflict and is probably the most readily resolved aspect of conflict. Then there is conflict that occurs because one or both parties simply want to fight, no matter about what. The conflict becomes a goal in itself, perhaps because it releases tension.

*Separate Goals from Interests.* There is an important theoretical – and practical – distinction between goals and interests. As we saw in Chapter 2, in a payoff matrix *goals* are the specific options (the rows of the payoff matrix) that have positive payoffs for the party. In practice, goals are usually perceived as the objectives of parties in a conflict. Sometimes the word "goals" is used to mean positions, specific demands being made by one party or the other: "If you wish to end the conflict, you must do this or that." Within the context of matrix conceptualization, *interests* are all of the outcomes (consequences) that have positive payoffs for the party. In practice, interests refer to certain nearly universally valued outcomes, that truly motivate the parties – something they really need to achieve: security, recognition, respect, justice, and so on (Burton 1990).

*Understand the Dynamics.* A conflict is constantly moving and changing. Even if parties are at a stalemate, some aspects of the conflict will be changing. Runaway responses (Coleman 1957) of parties to one another are made more visible through conflict mapping. Dynamics such as unrestrained escalation and polarization carry participants away from cooperative resolution toward greater hostility. Perception changes within the opposing sides reinforce the runaway responses: stereotyping opponents, seeing them as the negative mirror image of oneself, imputing to them increasingly sinister motives.

*Search for Positive Functions.* A "positive" function of a conflict is any consequence that has positive payoff for one or both of the parties. In some cases, the positive function may be openly pursued by a party, thus becoming its goal. In other cases, the positive function may be a release of tension or an aggressive impulse and may be only vaguely perceived. Thus a family struggle over finances may serve several functions: it may strengthen the wife's decision-making powers, make children more independent, induce the husband to take a more reasonable attitude toward his family. Knowing the positive functions often suggests ways – other than coercive conflict – by which the parties' goals can be reached.

*Understand the Regulation Potential.* Every conflict context contains its own conflict-limiting elements. There may be third parties that could intervene. Internal limiting factors such as the simple wish of the parties to maintain their relationship can be used. External limiting factors such as law and higher authority may be introduced.

# CHAPTER FIVE

# Emergence of Overt Conflicts

BEFORE December 7, 1941, relations between Japan and the United States were strained, but no overt hostilities existed. Then came the Japanese attack on Pearl Harbor, and the ensuing war between Japan and the United States. Why did the hidden hostilities change into an open war? Was it caused by the attack on Pearl Harbor?

Generally speaking, for an open conflict to emerge, two main conditions are needed: the formation of "conflict groups," and a sequence of events that ignites conflict action. Dahrendorf (1959) addressed the problem of conflict group formation in considerable detail. He argued that groups whose goals are incompatible but who do not realize it, will become full-scale conflict groups if each of them (1) has leaders committed to the conflict, (2) has a conflict ideology, (3) is free to organize for conflict, and (4) has members who can communicate with each other.[1] Dahrendorf's four conditions exist in groups that, in addition to having incompatible goals, have high conflict solidarity and sufficient conflict resources.

## Conflict Solidarity

We noted in Chapter 3 that free communication produces so-called communal values. But free communication can also promote conflict solidarity.

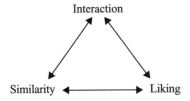

**Figure 5.1.** Homans's Theory of Free Communication

## Free Communication as a Cause of Solidarity

Sociologists usually distinguish between individuals who form a group and those who do not: if they interact with each other fairly regularly, they form a group; if they do not interact, they don't. For example, when families begin to move into a new housing development, they do not form a group as yet; but once they start talking and visiting, they become a "group."

Interaction is seen as a crucial ingredient of "groupness," not only because it establishes relationships between individuals but also because it tends to create features that are essential for a group's existence, such as group solidarity, identity, and culture. George Homans (1950; 1974) has developed a theory explaining how this happens.

Homans began by noting that, when members of a small group interact with each other freely, without being constrained by externally imposed norms or tasks, their interaction has unique consequences:[2] it increases their liking for each other and makes them similar in their actions, values, and beliefs. Moreover, as they become more similar and begin to like each other, their interaction increases further.

Figure 5.1 states that when a small group is without external restraints, the processes within it are of a special kind: interaction, similarity, and liking are bound together causally, so that when one increases, the others increase as well. For example, the arrow linking similarity and interaction can be translated as "The more the members interact with each other, the more similar they become in their values, beliefs, and action, and vice versa."[3] When you consider the full meaning of this figure, you begin to understand how solidarity is created.

To begin with, the figure helps us to *define* solidarity. We will say that a group has a high degree of solidarity if it possesses high levels of all three variables shown in Figure 5.1: *if its members interact with each other frequently, if they like each other, and if they hold similar beliefs, values, and norms.*

Moreover, Figure 5.1 suggests what *conditions* tend to increase solidarity. First, because solidarity will increase if free interaction increases, we should consider conditions that facilitate interaction. For example, because persons who live or work close to each other are more likely to interact than those far apart, it is usually easier to unionize steel workers who work in the same foundry than office staff scattered in different buildings. Another condition that favors high interaction – and therefore solidarity – is availability of certain communication technologies. For example, if all members of a group have telephones and e-mail addresses, it is easy for them to reinforce their common beliefs even if they live far apart.

But – and this condition is perhaps the most important – the group must be *small*, preferably no larger than about fifteen to twenty people (Berelson and Steiner 1964, 325), certainly not larger than fifty. For a group to develop high solidarity, each member must interact frequently with *all* other members, and this can occur only in small groups.

Homans's theory of free interaction and group solidarity is amply supported by empirical research. For example, the proposition that frequent interaction and similarity are related is supported by the fact that marriage occurs most frequently between those who are similar in race, religion, status, and education; the proposition that similarity and liking are related is supported by the finding that those with similar cultural backgrounds have happier marriages and are less likely to divorce than those with different backgrounds; and the proposition that interaction and liking are related is supported by the finding that those who live closest to one another (and hence are most likely to interact) are most likely to become friends. And the theory that the process of Figure 5.1 is related to group solidarity is supported by findings such as that residents of high-cohesion courts in a housing project were more likely to abide by the decisions of their community council than members of low-cohesion courts (Berelson and Steiner 1964, 305–306, 310–313, 328, and 332).

### *Hostility as a Cause of Conflict Solidarity*

Many conflicts have another ingredient that can fuel them and even change their character – hostility. Two main factors contribute to lasting hostility: specific grievances and a general feeling of frustration.

*Grievances.* You may be said to have a grievance if you believe that you have been treated unjustly (Kriesberg [1973] 1982, 67). Once members of a group believe that they have been treated unjustly by another group, they will begin to feel hostile toward that group. Many African Americans, because they were enslaved in the past, are hostile toward American whites whose ancestors were slaveholders; many Palestinians and Israelis feel hostility toward each other because each group occupies territory that at some point in history belonged to the other; many Irish Catholics hate Irish Protestants because parts of Ireland are controlled by the (mostly Protestant) British. Thus the same conditions that contribute to a sense of injustice and – as we saw in Chapter 3 – to goal incompatibility also create specific grievances that contribute to hostility.

*Frustration.* Whereas grievances usually target a specific group and are based on specific events, frustration tends to be expressed as free-floating hostility that can target almost anything at any time. The so-called frustration-aggression theory (Dollard et al. 1939) explains how frustration comes about. It holds that we become frustrated and feel hostile whenever we are prevented from reaching our goals. The important point is that, once we become frustrated without being able to vent our frustration through aggressive action, the feeling of frustration persists. If we continue to be frustrated without finding an outlet, the feeling becomes very intense and we may attack any person or group that is a handy target, even if it is not the source of our frustration.

Although frustration can be produced by the potential opponent, much of it has its source elsewhere. There is a sense in which almost all personal contacts are frustrating. When a wife wants to go out and have a good time, the husband may want to stay at home; when the husband wants to watch football on television, the wife may want to watch figure skating; when the husband wants to go and have a drink with his buddies, his wife may want him to stay home. And no matter how well the two manage to reach an agreement on what to do, one or both of them is frustrated because of not getting what he or she wanted.

In addition, there are "impersonal" – systemic – processes that are frustrating. One can be denied promotion, lose money in the stock market, be called by the school principal about the poor performance of one's child, or learn that one's favorite candidate has lost the election. It is possible to take all these misfortunes with outward calm, but inward pressure keeps on building.

### Conflict Solidarity and Conflict Ideology

For a group to become a conflict group, a certain type of solidarity is needed – conflict solidarity. The members must not only interact with each other, like each other, and share certain goals and values; their goal must be to engage in the conflict, and their values must support the struggle. In other words, they must develop a conflict culture or, as is often said, conflict *ideology*. To understand how it develops, we must understand how free interaction promotes the creation of any culture.

Free communication creates a common culture by "averaging" the beliefs, values, and expectations that the individual members bring into the group. This is illustrated by the classic experiments with the so-called autokinetic effect. When isolated subjects were placed in a completely dark room and shown a point of light that, in fact, was stationary, they saw it as moving, with the amount of motion varying widely from subject to subject. In the second set of experiments, the same subjects were placed together in small groups and were asked to repeat the task. In the group setting, individual perceptions converged to a common mean, with much less variation between them (Sherif 1936). Further research showed that the opinions of the leaders carried more weight than those of the followers. Thus a common view will always be skewed toward the opinions of the leaders.

Similarly, a culture may be viewed as an "average" of the opinions originally held by the members. To develop such culture, members must be free to communicate in small groups: neighbors talking across the fence, workers having a beer in a pub, college students talking in a dormitory room.

But most communications are not entirely free, because the members inevitably face some problems. When the problems are urgent and persistent, individual members will have ideas about how to solve them. And as they talk to each other about the problem, their ideas are "averaged" into social norms.[4] In preliterate tribes, the group members might develop rituals designed to bring about rain; in modern societies, members of a club might develop traditional ways of launching a membership drive.

When group members face a dangerous opponent, they tend to develop the needed "conflict ideology." But – and this point is crucial – ideologies cannot be imposed; they must evolve freely out of the opinions of individual members. This creates problems for leaders of large societies. Because free interaction can occur only in *small* groups, large societies have many relatively independent cultures, each specific to a group whose members have similar backgrounds. And the problem facing the leaders is how to alter the cultures of these subgroups so as to prepare them for conflict. For example, while President Roosevelt saw clearly that Nazi Germany was a threat to the United States, many groups in the United States refused to accept this as their own vision.

A device routinely used to achieve this end is the mass rally in which the opponent is portrayed as an enemy who poses a threat to every member of the group. But the effectiveness of this device is limited. For example, the mass rallies staged by the Nazis undoubtedly created great enthusiasm in the members of the audience – but this enthusiasm was short-lived if it was not shared by the participant's family and friends. As another example, consider Kerenski, a leader of Russia following the revolution of 1917. Although he was a great orator who kept his audience spellbound, he never had a great following because his views were not popular with ordinary Russians. He soon lost power to the Bolsheviks.

Let us repeat, then: for members of a group to create and adopt conflict ideology, two conditions must be met: individual members must be convinced that conflict is necessary, and they must meet in small groups to elevate their private beliefs into a binding group ideology.

*Conflict Solidarity and Organization*

Groups involved in short-lived conflicts are often driven by solidarity alone. For example, if some of the rioters are attacked by police, the rest will come to their rescue simply because they belong to the same group, not because the rescuers have been specially trained. Moreover, their leadership tends to shift from one member to the next, as the circumstances dictate. But members about to engage in a prolonged conflict need not only solidarity but also organization. How can a group develop such an organization if it is not already organized?

To begin with, unorganized groups develop organization – *any* kind of organization – by the same process they develop ideology: the ideas of individual members become averaged into generally accepted ideas, and these are converted into an organization. At the very least, members who are most respected or shown to be most adept at a particular task become the group's leaders. Thus American Indians often elected their bravest member to be their chief; members of a jury elect as chair the member they respect most. But many groups already have organization of some kind: church groups have their ministers, businesses their executives, governments their presidents. And these leaders have some organizational know-how.

They usually know much of what we discussed in Chapter 3. They know that, to engage in prolonged conflict, an organization should be differentiated both horizontally and vertically. And they develop units with a division of labor suited to the conflict – perhaps creating an army that is horizontally differentiated into units such as air force, artillery, and submarine forces, as well as vertically differentiated in a hierarchy ranging from privates to generals.

"Legitimate" industrial organizations tend to have permanent units that specialize in conflict. Governments have a police force for internal security and an army for external conflicts; universities, hospitals, museums, and factories have security forces at their disposal. Insurgent groups, on the other hand, tend to start without the benefit of any organization. Because the powerful will try to prevent them from organizing, they tend to go "underground": usually, they develop organizations with only minimal horizontal and vertical differentiation and with secret membership, with the rank-and-file members knowing only the members of their immediate unit. Whether the insurgents succeed in organizing more openly depends, in part, on the strength of those with power: the less mobilized for conflict the rulers are, the easier it is for the ruled to become organized (Dahrendorf 1959). When, in addition, the rulers lack solidarity, some of their members may defect and provide leadership for the ruled (see Brinton 1955).

As we saw in Chapter 3, most industrial organizations promote "system" values (see Table 3.1). But conflict organizations may promote some communal values as well. For example, although a soldier should be able to kill the opponent and tolerate the death of his friends (affective neutrality, a system value), he should also be patriotic and willing to sacrifice his life (particularism and collectivism, which are communal values). It should not surprise us that military solidarity is in fact fostered by small friendship groups rather than by the army itself, and that soldiers typically fight to gain respect from their friends and to protect them from the enemy (see Stouffer et al. 1949).

Some societies, such as small tribes, may be based exclusively on communal values. But, as Table 3.1 shows, some of these values may be inimical to the principles of a good organization. For example, how can a society in which all power is hereditary (and thus "ascriptive") create an organization led by the best-qualified members? And how can a society that values "diffusiveness" create a division of labor that presupposes specialization? The answer is that such societies may be unable to organize themselves for conflict and end up being victimized by their warlike neighbors. Those societies which succeed in developing an efficient conflict organization – such as the ancient Zulu kingdoms (Parsons 1977, 46) – may have accepted some of the values we now associate with industrial systems. For example, while they may emphasize bravery ("collectivism," a communal value), they may also train certain groups – such as adult men – to specialize in warfare ("specificity," a system value).

### Conflict Solidarity and Mobilization

Members of a group are not ready for conflict action unless they can mobilize sufficient resources and use them effectively. But, for a variety of reasons, they may not be motivated to participate in the conflict. An important reason is that they may be seduced into "free riding" (see, e.g., Olson 1965; Hechter 1987), a behavior that occurs when it is advantageous for them *not* to participate. For example, a union member is free-riding if he or she, while willing to enjoy all the benefits of a new contract, refuses to go on strike and join the picket lines. This problem is difficult to solve, primarily because free riding is often very rational from the point of view of an individual member. Why should a worker incur the cost of a conflict if he or she can enjoy its benefits in any case?

Research suggests that free riding exists primarily in groups whose members have dissimilar goals (Blalock 1989, 52–56). But recall that, as it creates group solidarity, free interaction also promotes acceptance of common goals. Thus solidarity automatically replaces individualistic values (which make free riding rational) with collectivistic values (which demand sacrifice). And leaders can overcome the free-riding problem if they succeed in promoting group solidarity. But, as we mentioned earlier, this is not an easy task to accomplish.

## Conflict Resources

What constitutes a conflict resource varies: to wage a war, a nation needs (in addition to conflict organization) soldiers,[5] weapons, and ammunition; to start a strike, a union needs (in addition to high solidarity) personnel to walk picket lines, picket signs, and money; to start divorce proceedings against her husband, a wife needs financial security and a lawyer; to disagree with what is being said during a meeting, a participant should have both support from friends and the ability to "speak powerfully" (Lulofs and Cahn 2000, 143).

But, even when these resources are available, the conflict group may not have mobilized enough of them. For example, a police force may have enough men and women to handle routine problems but not enough to handle a major disturbance. When a major riot occurs, it may have not only to cancel all leaves but also to ask for help from the National Guard. Thus to start a conflict action, an actor should have enough resources to sustain the action and ultimately reach his or her goal.

## Typical Beginnings

Just how open conflicts begin varies: some start suddenly, others develop gradually; some start violently, others moderately. And yet, as Kriesberg ([1973] 1982; 1998) has argued, some regularities merit attention.

### Early Warning Signs

Once conflict groups are created, there may be ample evidence that an open conflict is imminent. One of these is the very fact of mobilization: by calling in the reserves, a nation signals that it expects an open conflict. Although this signal may be inadvertent, in many cases it is deliberate: mobilization may be used as a show of strength, intended to intimidate the opponent.

But the preconflict period may also include serious – and not so serious – attempts at cooperation, with the adversaries trying to persuade or reward each other. Thus before Japanese planes attacked Pearl Harbor, Japan and the United States were engaged in delicate and seemingly promising negotiations. And, in the infamous Munich Conference of 1938, the Western Allies tried to prevent a major war with Hitler by giving him a substantial part of Czechoslovakia.

### The Spark That Ignites

In spite of attempts at cooperation, once conflict groups are created, an open conflict is likely. An outbreak may happen for seemingly insignificant reasons: because a roommate did not close the door properly; because a man did not like the way another man looked at him; because a member of a community was arrested for a routine transgression; because a nation's compatriots living in a foreign country were verbally abused by that country's government. Clearly these minor events would not start conflict behavior if the actors were not ready for it – if they did not have incompatible goals or were not hostile toward each other. However, these "insignificant" events – these new grievances – are equally important, because without them the conflict might not start. Thus urban riots are often started when a rumor about police brutality spreads through a minority community. The illegal Japanese attack on Pearl Harbor created a great deal of animosity against the Japanese and made it possible for Roosevelt to declare war on Japan.[6]

It does not make much difference that the rumor is often false. In fact, politicians may create false rumors to discredit their opponents. For example, Hitler in 1939 gained support for his intended invasion of Poland by circulating reports about Polish brutalities against Germans, brutalities that he himself had secretly staged. What matters is that the rumor is believed, and that it comes at the right time, when the actors are ready for a conflict.

### The Attack

Open hostilities often begin with the adversaries playing different roles: one is the attacker, the other the defender. In some cases, the attack is sudden and violent, and gives the attacker the benefit of surprise. Thus when the Japanese unexpectedly attacked Pearl Harbor in 1941, they succeeded beyond their expectations. In other cases, the attacker starts rather innocuously, becoming violent later. For example, in the late 1940s the Soviet Union, determined to block the reunification of Germany, started by merely protesting any attempts at reunification. When this did not work, it adopted increasingly coercive actions: it began to interrupt communication between Berlin and West Germany and ended with a blockade of the city (Pruitt and Rubin 1986, 90).

But, in the long run, the difference between the attacker and the defender disappears as the adversaries begin to behave in a similar fashion, each attacking, retaliating, and (possibly) retreating.

### Conclusions

Members of groups with incompatible goals are likely to engage in an open conflict if they become conflict groups. Open conflict is likely to occur if the members are aware that their goals are incompatible with those of the opposing group, if they have grievances against opponents and feel very frustrated, if they engage in free interaction that favors conflict action, and if they have sufficient resources. But by far the two

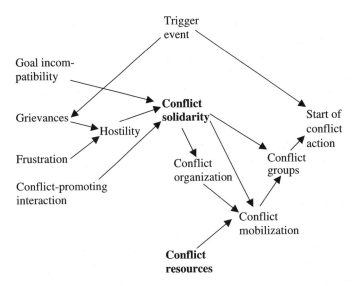

**Figure 5.2.** Causes That Lead to Open Conflicts

most important variables are conflict solidarity and conflict resources:
a group will become a conflict group *if it acquires both high conflict
solidarity and sufficient conflict resources* (see Figure 5.2).

The needed *conflict solidarity* is not easily achieved. The difficulty
stems from the fact that to reach it, group members must be free to
interact without any constraints, and yet their interaction must create conflict ideology. This problem is most likely to be solved when
the members not only recognize that their goals are incompatible
with those of their opponents, but also have many grievances against
them and are frustrated. Under these conditions, their free interaction
facilitates conflict and, in time, produces the needed conflict
solidarity.

Although the availability of *conflict resources* plays a crucial role, the
group's conflict solidarity also contributes significantly to the creation
of an efficient organization and motivates the members to mobilize the
needed resources. The *actual beginning* of a conflict is often preceded
by some early warning signs. Some of them are unintentional, such as
sudden mobilization of reserves; others are intentional, such as threats.
In some cases, the adversaries even make a last-ditch effort to avoid
open conflict. But when all of the factors shown in Figure 5.2 are in

place, it may be too late; all that is needed now is a trigger event, and open conflict begins.

As an addendum to our main argument, let us note that the theory of Figure 5.2 accounts for Dahrendorf's four conditions of conflict group formation. It shows that, once it is clear that the goals are incompatible, free communication (his condition number 4) is quite likely to create conflict ideology (condition number 2), and that each group is likely to become organized for conflict (condition number 3) and to develop leadership committed to the conflict (condition number 1).

## Application to Interpersonal Conflicts

Because the theory presented in this chapter focuses on the creation of conflict *groups*, it might seem that it is not applicable to a conflict between individuals. Actually, this is not so: with a few modifications, it is directly applicable to interpersonal conflicts as well.

Certain aspects of the theory shown in Figure 5.2 can be applied without change: individuals can have incompatible goals, have grievances against each other, and be frustrated. Other concepts have to be modified: an individual cannot develop conflict solidarity or conflict organization, or coalesce into a conflict group. What he can do is acquire some properties suggested by these concepts.

Although an individual in conflict cannot develop conflict solidarity, she can get ready by creating an equivalent: she can work herself up to a high emotional pitch. She cannot interact with members of a nonexistent conflict group but can talk to herself, mentally rehearsing her arguments. For example, a tenant about to confront her landlord might work up a head of steam by repeating to herself all her grievances: that, in spite of repeated requests, the landlord did not fix the leaking faucets nor did he heat her apartment sufficiently. And she may rehearse several times the speech she will give: "I have been patient for a long time, but I want some action and want it now. I do want to have good relations with you, but if you do not follow through, I will have no choice but . . ." Thus the tenant can prepare herself not only for a conflict generally but also for a specific conflict action.

# CHAPTER SIX

# Application to a University Conflict

SOMETIMES a conflict results not so much from direct discrimination and prejudice, as in the case of the civil rights movement, as it does from established ways of evaluating performance and from honest disagreement over standards and procedures to be used. In an organization, those disagreements can combine with friendship patterns, putting those who are without such ties – such as minority and women faculty – at a considerable disadvantage. They cannot benefit equally from membership in the "old boys network" or from long-standing and inflexible standards of evaluation. The result is what is commonly known as institutional racism and sexism. Here we use a conflict in a university to illustrate the theory developed in Chapter 5. Although in this chapter we focus on how a hidden conflict became open, we need to prepare the ground first by giving a brief synopsis and then by considering why the goals of the two parties in this chapter's conflict were incompatible.

## Goal Incompatibility

For the necessary data for our analysis, let us describe briefly the early history of an actual faculty tenure conflict at a university in the western United States.

### Short History

Top administrators had been trying for some years to lift the university into the top rank of research universities in the nation. Standards for faculty promotion and tenure had consequently been tightening and becoming more narrowly academic. At the same time, recruitment and retention of women and minority faculty had also become a major goal of the university. Minority faculty members sensed that they were at an unjust disadvantage: while they were expected to promote the university's public image and increase its ethnic diversity through work with minority issues and communities, any teaching and research they did in that direction was discounted under the widely accepted – but rather narrow – standards of "academic excellence."

This latent conflict situation took concrete form in the promotion and tenure case of a Chicano sociologist. When the department recommended against his tenure, charges of personal and institutional racism were made by the three Chicano department members, citing a "racist" department chair, a "hostile atmosphere" in the department, and "irregular" voting procedures. Minority students quickly organized protest rallies, marches to offices of top administrators, and press releases charging unfair treatment of minorities throughout the campus. The recommendation to deny tenure was subsequently upheld by two higher administrative committees. It was appealed to the president, however, who reversed it. After tenure was granted by the regents, the Chicano sociologists all requested and received transfers to other departments.

### Theoretical Analysis

There is ample evidence suggesting that the goals of the Chicano faculty and those of the remaining sociology faculty were incompatible. A substantial majority of the sociology department voted against granting tenure to the Chicano professor, whereas, as their appeals demonstrated, the Chicano faculty members wished that tenure be awarded. To establish why the goals of the Chicanos and many of the sociology faculty were incompatible, let us return to the theory presented in Figure 3.2.

Let us consider which of the three direct causes of goal incompatibility – contested resources, incompatible roles, and incompatible values – played a major role in the conflict within the department of sociology.

*Were the Resources Contested?* The Chicanos argued that resources were not distributed fairly at the university. They showed statistically that ethnic minorities were not proportionately represented among the faculty (power); they argued that the departmental budget was not allocated fairly (wealth); and they claimed that they were treated in a condescending and discriminatory fashion (prestige).

It appears that the main reason for their complaint was a sense of injustice, and that this feeling was fueled both by *relative deprivation* and by a belief that the chair exercised his power in *illegitimate* ways (the "irregular" voting procedure). Because the Chicanos did not say that their resources were insufficient for doing their work, "absolute" deprivation was not a major cause of the complaint.

As usually happens with injustice, those who fought it at the university sometimes saw it where others saw none. For example, while the chair is expected to be helpful to his faculty, one of the Chicano faculty saw the chair's offers of help as condescending and discriminatory. This suggests that personal or cultural belligerence – another possible reason for disputing the distribution of resources (see Figure 3.2) – was also contributing to the conflict.

*Were the Roles Incompatible?* Both vertical and horizontal role differentiation played a part in the conflict. The *horizontal* (between equals) differentiation was influential in that the Chicano faculty specialized in the study of Chicano communities, institutions, culture, and movements. They argued that, because their field of study was unique, they had to use a unique mix of research methods and that, therefore, the standards of academic excellence used by their colleagues (such as publication in certain prestigious journals) were not broad enough to allow fair evaluation of their work.

*Vertical* differentiation was also responsible. Feeling that he was representing the interests of the discipline of sociology, the chair argued that the department must consider the interests of the discipline as a whole, and that certain common standards for evaluation must be followed by all regardless of their area of specialization. The Chicanos, on the other hand, defended their special interests, the study of and advocacy for the Chicano community.

*Were the Values Incompatible?* It can also be argued that the conflict was due to value differences, and that to a large extent these differences were related to the community-system dichotomy we discussed in Chapter 3. This was revealed when the Chicano faculty used the argument – often advanced by minorities – that the criteria for promotion used by the department were not universal, that they were the overly narrow standards of white European men. We may reinterpret this argument and say that the department of sociology and its chair were using standards consistent with the *industrial system* (which indeed originated in a Europe ruled by white men). These standards implicitly accepted the values listed in the right column of Table 3.1: researchers should be affectively neutral, relying on objective methods such as statistical analysis; they should be self-oriented in that they alone should determine the course of research, without consulting their subjects; they should be universalistic, treating all of their subjects in the same manner, disregarding whatever personal ties they might have with some of them and ignoring their ascribed qualities such as sex, race, and ethnicity; and they should be specialists in one of the established fields of the discipline of sociology, such as criminology, family studies, or sociology of religion.

On the other hand, the teaching and research of the Chicano faculty member who was being considered for tenure seem to have reflected heavily the *communal values* listed in the left column of Table 3.1. In the classroom, he promoted emotional involvement through techniques such as having students hold hands; he studied the Chicano community in an informal, intuitive, nonstatistical manner; he published articles that were noted more for their advocacy of Chicano advancement than for their objective distance; he published more often in local newspapers than in professional journals.

### Conclusions

The sources of the university conflict are represented in Figure 6.1. Note that, unlike the civil rights conflict, the university conflict involved all three direct causes. The first of these, contested distribution of resources, played a major role: the Chicanos felt that the denial of tenure was unjust, a part of systematic discrimination against minorities. The parties had different and incompatible goals also because

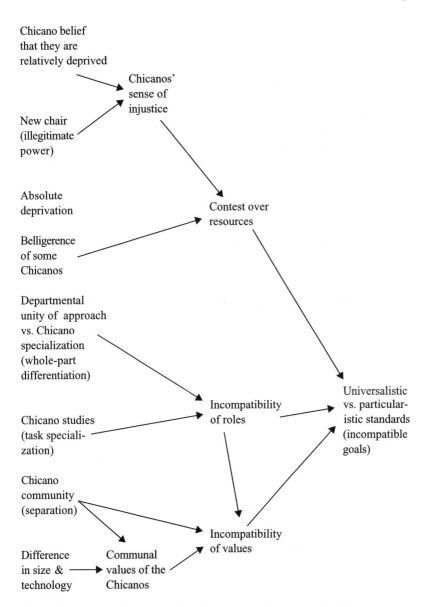

**Figure 6.1.** Causes of Incompatible Goals in the University Conflict

they played different roles. The chair of the sociology department defended what he saw as the interests of the discipline as a whole, the Chicanos defended the interests of Chicano studies. Finally, the goal incompatibility was also due to value differences. The majority of the department and its chair defended the values of the industrial system, such as universalism; the Chicano professors defended the legitimacy of teaching and research reflecting the particularistic values inherent in communities. Figure 6.1 also shows that only one of the "exogenous" causes was without significant influence.[1] The Chicano faculty members were not "absolutely" deprived, because they had sufficient resources for their research and a decent standard of living.

## Emergence of Overt Conflict

Having considered why the goals of the two parties were incompatible, we turn to the main topic of this chapter: how can the theory of Chapter 5 be used to explain how a latent conflict became an open one?

### Relevant History

Often, a major conflict within an organization produces smaller, more localized conflicts. In our case, the university as a whole was ripe for a governance crisis at the time of the tenure dispute. There was an ongoing conflict between the faculty and the president, who had been appointed several years earlier by the board of regents without real consultation with the faculty. When that conflict became public, the university entered a period of deep political and administrative uncertainty. The legitimacy of power, and decision-making competence at all administrative levels, had been called into question both within and beyond the university. An atmosphere of doubt pervaded its flagship campus where the conflict was centered.

It was within this setting that the Chicano sociologist had come up for tenure. Although his department had voted, earlier in the year, to reappoint a Chicana member, they now voted by a two-thirds majority not to recommend tenure for him and sent their decision up the administrative hierarchy. None of the three Chicano faculty in the department had good relations with the outspoken and inexperienced department chair. There were some minor irregularities in the voting on the tenure case, but under normal circumstances they would probably have been easily straightened out. These, however, were not normal times. The three Chicanos charged the department with having a "racially hostile atmosphere," directing their accusation at the chair in particular.

Believing that their goals of fair and equal treatment were not being met, the Chicano sociologists began to mobilize support for an anticipated struggle with the department and higher administrators. Chicano students and some Chicano faculty colleagues in other departments joined the conflict group. The media, already focused on the university's problems, quickly labeled this episode as simply another dimension of those problems. Direct action to disrupt business as usual, something that all leaders of bureaucratic organizations dread, took the form of student rallies, press conferences, and march-ins. A good deal of solidarity was produced in those direct action settings. The conflict group probably gained more power during that period of institutional vulnerability than it would have under more normal conditions.

The Chicanos' opponents, however, did not become a close-knit conflict group. Most members of the sociology department, though divided on the tenure question, supported their chair. They felt that, while he could have handled the process more tactfully and carefully, he was not a racist and was an obvious scapegoat for minority unhappiness with established procedures that contributed to institutional racism. Furthermore, the department had been directed by university administrators, who expected lawsuits, not to respond publicly to charges. It could defend itself only in private conversations and through the procedure of administrative inquiry. The department could at best be described as an unwilling and unmobilized conflict group, though some increased solidarity did result as it hunkered down to ride out a storm it felt was not of its own making.

The tenure decision made its way through the university. The original recommendation to deny tenure was accepted by the campus chancellor, normally the final authority in the process. The Chicano sociologist requested that the president review the denial of tenure. Several prominent figures outside the university who were asked to review the conflict and to submit recommendations concluded that neither the chair nor the department was guilty of racist behavior, but that institutional racism was operating nevertheless. Moreover, they saw the chair as inexperienced and unnecessarily outspoken.

The president of the university reversed the chancellor's decision and recommended tenure, which was approved by the regents. The Chicano faculty asked to be transferred to other departments, and their requests were granted; the chair of the department decided not to seek another term.

### Theoretical Analysis

The evidence shows that tensions within the department of sociology erupted into an open conflict. The Chicano faculty filed numerous complaints about the procedure whereby tenure was denied, and they made statements to the press about the climate of racial hostility within the department. Their allies among the students staged demonstrations and verbally attacked the chair of the department. The conflict action on the part of the department was more subdued, consisting primarily in standing by its decision and defending itself in personal conversations against the charges of racism.

In order to explain why the conflict became open, we employ the theory developed in Chapter 5 and summarized in Figure 5.2. Let us consider whether the two parties coalesced into two opposing conflict groups. To accomplish this, we shall examine the three main causes that can lead to the formation of conflict groups: conflict solidarity, conflict organization, and conflict mobilization.

*Did Conflict Solidarity Increase?* Figure 5.2 suggests that, once the goals are perceived as incompatible, an increase in group solidarity often consolidates individuals into conflict groups and converts disagreements between the groups into an open conflict. The three Chicano sociologists and their allies had at least two of the ingredients identified in Figure 5.2 as necessary for solidarity building: they met frequently (interaction), and they developed justifications for and a commitment to the goal of reversing the tenure decision (conflict ideology). Moreover, they displayed considerable hostility toward their opponents: the three Chicano members refused to attend departmental meetings; they made accusations against the department that were deemed excessive by an independent review panel; and their student allies harassed the chair of the department.

Figure 5.2 suggests two possible reasons for this increased hostility: new grievances and general frustration. The Chicano faculty members certainly felt that they had *grievances* against the department. They saw the denial of tenure as simply new evidence in a history of discrimination. Furthermore, having lived in a state of cultural marginality, they must have had an intense sense of *frustration*.[2] As this case history suggests, the university-wide conflict – around topics such as higher academic standards and hiring and promotion of minorities – created forces outside the department that increased their frustration and created additional grievances. But that wider conflict also opened for them the opportunity structure that enabled them and other challenge groups to advance their cause in the university and the community. In this case, tenure was awarded, standards have become somewhat broader, and minority rights were protected.

Other members of the sociology faculty were much less successful in increasing their solidarity. True, there were some meetings, and some increase in hostility expressed towards the Chicanos as the conflict evolved. But the chair received little support from the administration, other departments, or the larger community.

*Did the Groups Become Organized for Conflict?* Because the conflict was short-lived, only minimal organization occurred within the Chicano group. Some vertical differentiation occurred: the three Chicano sociologists served as leaders who provided guidance for their less powerful allies at the university and in the community. Some horizontal specialization occurred as well: some persons addressed student demonstrators, whereas others gave interviews to the press and television. But this organization was very tentative, and role assignment was subject to change. Thus it cannot be said that a clear-cut conflict organization emerged and contributed to making the conflict overt.

The remaining sociology faculty relied on the formal organization of the department: the chair, the various committees, and departmental meetings (which the Chicano members stopped attending). However, this organization was handicapped when it came to the conflict, both because higher administration discouraged the chair and members from making public statements and because the solidarity of this group was low. Thus there did not develop a conflict-specific organization of the sociology department.

*Did the Groups Mobilize Their Resources?* The Chicano sociologists had sufficient material and human resources and were successful in mobilizing them. They acquired powerful allies: minority students and faculty, the media, and, ultimately, the president of the university. The remaining sociology faculty was less successful in gaining overt support. However, the university faculty generally criticized the president for overruling the recommendations of the three committees that reviewed the request for tenure.

### Conclusions

There were many reasons why the goals of the two parties were incompatible. As an independent review of the department later concluded, although there was no evidence of discrimination by persons, there was institutional discrimination – and hence injustice – within the department. There were differing perceptions of the Chicano sociologists' roles: the chair wanted them to behave like conventional scholars, whereas the Chicanos wanted to do research useful for the Chicano community. The Chicanos tended to give more importance to the values of the community, the majority of the sociology faculty to the values of the industrial system.

Similarly, several causes contributed to making the conflict open. There was a high level of interaction within the Chicano community; there were grievances, past and present; and there was a high level of frustration. Moreover, the presidential crisis added external pressures on the department and new opportunity for the challengers.

Although a single diagram can usually represent goal incompatibility,[3] two figures are often needed to show the causes of an overt conflict action, one for the initiator, one for the defender. Because the defenders in this conflict (the non-Chicano sociologists) simply react to the initiators (the Chicano sociologists), their action is best considered as "escalation," a process to be considered in Chapters 7 and 8.[4] Because the initiators start the overt conflict, their action needs to be explained, and we do so with Figure 6.2. Once again, we use terminology favorable to the Chicano initiators.

Observe that we added two causes not mentioned in the original theory of Figure 5.2: the denial of tenure and the university-wide conflict. Such additions are often necessary when a general theory is applied

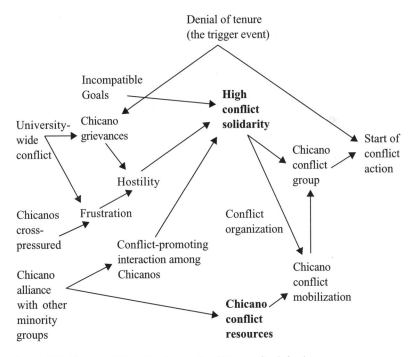

**Figure 6.2.** Causes of Conflict Action by Chicano Sociologists

to a specific case, and they do not invalidate the theory. Note also that, of the possible causes listed in Figure 6.2, all but one (organization) contributed to the emergence of open conflict.

## Making Conflict Emergence Productive

The conflict was costly for both sides. The three Chicano sociologists lost good friends in the department and ended in faculty positions they originally did not seek. The remaining members of the department lost not only their Chicano friends but also their sense of collegiality with other faculty and administrators outside the department, whose lack of support they resented, and ultimately lost an outstanding sociologist when their chair resigned largely as a consequence of the conflict. Were these costs necessary? We think not. We believe that members of conflict groups can become more aware of how their group is forming and for what purposes, and that they can consciously make the conflict more productive and less costly. And the more contained the conflict, the easier it is for conflict groups to shape it to their advantage.

### Goals and Interests

What is it that our conflict group is really after, and how best do we get it? That is the primary question members should consistently ask as the group forms. The process of setting goals and constantly reviewing them as the conflict emerges is very important yet rarely done properly. Is our goal reasonably achievable? Should we be first seeking an interim goal that will lead to the ultimate one? Gamson's (1990, 149) research suggests that in U.S. history conflict groups with limited goals have been much more successful than those seeking broad systemic changes.

A group should distinguish its goals from its public positions – what it really wants from what it tells its opponents it must have. We are convinced that conflict groups empower themselves more through goal clarification and sound strategizing than they do through presentation of demands and posturing. The two approaches, however, may not be mutually exclusive. For low-power conflict groups, such as the minority faculty in our university case, publicizing demands and positions through the media may be sound strategizing for attaining an important intermediate goal: directing public attention to a legitimate grievance. The question then becomes how to phrase one's position to engage one's constituents' emotions and support sufficiently without moving one's opponent to resistance that will be costly to overcome.

Conflict groups should identify those goals that are truly incompatible with their opponent's and shape their conflict action accordingly. Degree of incompatibility is important to know as well. Goals that are somewhat compatible might lead to cooperation with opponents and to desired change; totally incompatible goals, on the other hand, can be a basis of conflict action to get opponents to modify their goals.

First, however, the conflict group should use the procedure we have described here and in Chapters 3 and 4 to determine why certain goals are incompatible. This will help them to determine their strategy and tactics. If contested resources were the source of incompatibility, they might consider what redistribution might be acceptable. If role differentiation was the origin, they might consider redefining some of the roles. If values differences were the root cause, they might seek a solution that is consistent with both sets of values. In the tenure decision case, for example, either side might have suggested that educating university students in the most diverse way was a common and thus compatible goal. They could then have collaborated to develop a teaching curriculum and research agenda and evaluation standards sufficiently flexible to be both fair and productive. The university administration might furthermore have suspended the tenure-granting procedure in the case in point until the issue was cooperatively resolved.

Our observation is that conflict groups, challengers and challenged alike, too quickly take coercive action toward their opponents, without considering the full range of options available to them. Ultimatums and nonnegotiable positions tend to throw the switch toward the wrong track. Coercive action should be the last – not first – step in a conflict. Force and threat are especially risky actions within organizations, because organizations depend on a high degree of interdependence of roles and cooperation among persons. Nevertheless, it is particularly difficult for low-power groups (who need to dramatize and publicize the conflict) and bureaucratic organizations such as universities (which are run by inflexible rules) to resist going down the coercive track first. It should be added that, in this conflict, high-level administrators were as deficient in using rational and cooperative conflict skills as were those below them.

### Organization and Mobilization of Resources for Empowerment

As conflict groups clarify their goals, they should identify resources to achieve those goals. They should organize their members and mobilize the power they have or could get. Unfortunately, many conflict groups assess their resources, such as their potential allies, in an unorganized and ineffective way. Moreover, they also tend to antagonize some neutral groups by adopting a belligerent approach or style of conflict. Conflict groups should be much more concerned about not creating new opponents than they usually are. A conflict group that early in its formation does a thorough inventory of its power resources, including potential allies and opponents, will be more successful than one that does not. Some rather frenzied and unorganized resource mobilization occurred on both sides in the university conflict, in the form of petitions, letters of support, hastily called mass meetings, and media spin doctoring. There is much to be said for slowing down the conflict, thus permitting more careful mobilization of resources and careful identification of compatible and incompatible goals.

Conflict groups usually wait until late in the conflict before they consider the possibility that neutral third parties might work with them to mediate away some of their differences. A conflict group can increase its power by reducing those differences through negotiation and mediation, then concentrating its resources on the tougher residual issues.[5] Intermediaries – and specialists who create dispute resolution systems for organizations – normally place third-party potential at the center of their proposed design (Ury, Brett, and Goldberg 1993).

As conflict groups form, the question of visibility looms large. What are the relative costs and benefits of high visibility? When is the public stage useful and when does it hinder a group's cause? When are the news media a conflict group's allies and when not? Often a conflict action may achieve one of the group's goals but deny it another. The Chicano faculty group in the university conflict made ample use of media coverage. This helped it to reach its goal of reversing the tenure decision. However, publicity also made it harder for the nonminority faculty to join the Chicanos in their struggle.

### Conflict Group Integration

As the theorist Georg Simmel ([1908] 1955) has observed, a group's sense of solidarity and oneness is often a function of its opposition to an out-group. The real challenge for a conflict group is to develop sufficient group consciousness and solidarity to motivate its members without generating excessive hostility toward the opponent. If the adversaries become too hostile, too threatening toward one another, violence and other destructive consequences will occur, and the accommodation ultimately required of them will become very difficult to achieve. The university tenure conflict illustrates this point: strident, threatening, and abusive language, particularly in public settings, created in-group solidarity but made between-group accommodation difficult.

How integrated the conflict groups are internally and how intense the conflict between them is depends on how well they communicate.

Successful groups communicate accurately both internally and externally.

### Strategies during Conflict Emergence

A successful conflict group determines the proper mix of different types of power to use with its opponent. It wishes to get its opponent to do something or to stop doing it – in the case of the civil rights struggle to give blacks equal respect, or in the university case to award tenure to a Chicano professor. As we saw in Chapter 2, a group in conflict has four main action options: to coerce the opponents with threats or use of force; to reward them through "side payments" (such as trading acts of cooperation or according each other respect); to persuade them by bringing to their attention some benefits of change they failed to see; or to search for a new and mutually acceptable solution. A conflict group should use a mix of all four. Often, as open conflict emerges, it uses coercion, then shifts to negotiation that reallocates rewards, and finally uses persuasion and a joint search to reach an accommodation.

But this may not always be the best approach: the particular mix a group should use often depends on the amount and type of power it has at a given moment. Conscious strategizing should lead to a mix of conflict actions that suits both the current stage of conflict and the group's resources (Wehr, Burgess, and Burgess 1994, 81–98). In our tenure conflict, had the department's leadership not already been locked into a coercive mode, and had its members been more imaginative, the sociology faculty might have made an "alternative procedure" proposal to higher administrators. The latter might have been receptive to such an approach, which would have deferred the conflict so as to avoid entangling it with their larger conflict with the president. Such an approach would have combined reward and persuasion power, a potentially disarming strategic mix that the Chicano faculty might have found hard to resist.

But this is hindsight. Skillful as we may be in controlling how conflict emerges, the conflict process always seems to take on a life of its own. Disruptive dynamics like escalation and polarization often chase out reflection and reason as the conflict develops.

# CHAPTER SEVEN

# Escalation and Deescalation

AN ISRAELI army jeep patrols the streets of Hebron in occupied Palestine. It has been doing this for months, without incident. But today things go differently. Suddenly, a crowd of young Palestinians starts throwing rocks at the jeep. The Israeli soldiers respond with gunfire. Several youths are wounded. And an upward spiral of violence is begun. Why?

Answers to this question cannot be found in the writings of classical theoreticians. Although they spent considerable effort on the fundamental causes of conflict, they were, by and large, uninterested in its dynamics.[1] Much more relevant for us are modern writers such as Coleman (1957), Deutsch (1973), Pruitt and Rubin (1986), and Kriesberg (1998). Their writings suggest that certain fundamental – and controversial – aspects of escalation need to be considered first.

## Main Ingredients of Escalation

We may begin by asking a deceptively simple question. What makes conflict escalation different from processes considered so far? And the answer is again seemingly simple: the fact that there are two (or more) contestants – the "Party" and the "Opponent" – who *interact* with each other. This fact is of crucial theoretical importance, because it suggests that Party's escalation is driven by *two* separate forces: one that originates within the Party itself, the other that originates in its Opponent.

The first force may be called "unilateral" escalation (or deescalation), the other "reciprocated" escalation (or deescalation). Let us begin by considering how these two forces contribute to the intensification of the conflict.

## Unilateral Escalation

A Party may wish to escalate *unilaterally* for any of the reasons we discussed in Chapter 3. It may escalate because it has been deprived, relatively or absolutely, by its Opponent; because it has a belligerent culture or personality; because it plays a role that is incompatible with that of the Opponent; or because its values are different from the Opponent's (see Figure 3.2). Unilateral escalation can also occur for reasons discussed in Chapter 5, such as past and present grievances, high level of frustration, or conflict-promoting interaction (see Figure 5.2).

But Party can also escalate because, under certain circumstances, escalation is *rational.* For example, when Party has *overwhelming* power over its opponent, it makes sense to use it to overcome Opponent's resistance. In some cases, overwhelming power is used at the very beginning of the struggle. For example, when the Germans attacked Poland in 1939, they used every destructive means at their disposal, including devastating bombing of civilian targets. In other cases, power is applied mercilessly to subdue lasting resistance. And, sad to say, such ruthlessness often pays – perhaps because Opponent, thinking rationally, concludes that resistance is useless. For example, when the Nazis annihilated the village of Lidice following the assassination by Czech patriots of Heindrich, the Nazi governor of Czechoslovakia, the Czechs were frightened by this savagery and concluded that extreme acts of violence against the Germans were not in their best interests.

But extreme force, though effective in the short run, might ultimately backfire. Particularly when it takes an unacceptable form, it may anger the opponents, thereby increasing their solidarity and, ultimately, their power. Familiar with this principle, savvy politicians often try to provoke their more powerful opponents. For example, Fidel Castro advanced his revolution against the Batista regime by attacking small army units and provoking the government into harsh reprisals. This strategy was successful, increasing Castro's following and resulting in his victory. On the other hand, rational parties can refuse to be provoked. For example, when Che Guevara tried Castro's approach in Venezuela, the government used only specific and limited countermeasures. The insurrection failed (Kriesberg [1973] 1982, 203).

### Reciprocated Escalation

Retaliation is a special case of reciprocation: it contributes to escalation (whereas reciprocation may drive deescalation as well), and it often involves greater violence than used by Opponent (whereas reciprocation usually matches Opponent's violence). In spite of these differences, retaliation is driven by the same forces as reciprocation.

Retaliation (and, more broadly, reciprocation) often occurs for the same reasons as unilateral escalation. It may be due to the distant past, such as an injustice inflicted on one's ancestors; it may be based on Opponent's recent actions, such as his latest atrocity; it may occur because the actor is rational, such as when he or she has overwhelming power over his or her adversary; or it may be due to his or her belligerent ideology or personality.

Although identifying the main causes of retaliation is relatively easy, specifying its *consequences* is much more difficult. Does it invite further retaliation? Or does it promote submission? Results of empirical studies are inconclusive. Some research suggests that escalation invites retaliation. For example, when in the 1960s college administrators responded to students' antiwar demonstrations by applying severe sanctions, the conflicts tended to escalate (Morgan 1977). Other research suggests quite the opposite. For example, highly coercive regimes tend to have lower levels of internal conflict than regimes that are only moderately coercive (Walton 1970).

In order to explain these seemingly inconsistent findings, let us make two observations. First, retaliation seems to be a "normal" and automatic reaction. As Coleman (1957, 13) puts it, "If you fail to smile, but scowl instead, I may say a harsh word; you respond in kind, and another chain of mutual reinforcement builds up – this time toward antagonism. . . . The admonition to 'turn the other cheek' is not easily obeyed." The tendency to retaliate becomes even more entrenched when it is culturally sanctioned. Thus the Old Testament demands "an eye for an eye, a tooth for a tooth" – and the Israeli government often uses this rule as a guide for its national policy. Many cultures, including mainstream U.S. culture, emphasize and sanction the positive side of reciprocation: when somebody does me a favor, I should return it.

Second, reciprocation (and sometimes retaliation) seems eminently *rational* under certain circumstances. For example, the so-called tit-for-tat strategy, recommended by some versions of the so-called theory of games (see Luce and Raiffa 1967; Axelrod 1984), relies heavily on reciprocation: when Opponent escalates, Party should escalate; when he or she deescalates, Party should deescalate as well. But this version of the tit-for-tat strategy does not stop there: it also specifies that, occasionally, *Party* should *deescalate unilaterally.* As the Sicilian vendetta illustrates, reciprocation locks the adversaries into a never-ending conflict that cannot be terminated unless somebody takes the first step toward reconciliation. Nonetheless, reciprocation is both natural and, under most circumstances, rational.

Hence we propose the following view of retaliation. Most fundamentally, retaliation should be viewed as a *natural,* spontaneous, and often irrational response to coercion. This natural human tendency, however, coexists with another, *rational* deliberation. In some instances, the two forces are in harmony, but in other cases they are in opposition. And in some cases, such as when facing overwhelming power, rationality wins. These cases should be viewed as evidence that, when the pressure is on, reason often overwhelms – but never extinguishes – nature.

Thus use of force can have two different consequences: when it is relatively *weak,* it tends to provoke retaliation; when it is *overpowering,* it tends to induce submission. But we must always remember that the use of extreme force may backfire in the long run.

Let us take a moment to consider a related issue – the controversy about the so-called realistic perspective on foreign affairs (Morgenthau 1960). According to that perspective, a state should be viewed as a rational actor that uses force to maximize its power. And the best way for a state to prevent war with its neighbors is to become much more powerful than they are. This theory has been opposed on many grounds. One of them is that when a state attempts to increase its power, its neighbors are likely to reciprocate by increasing theirs, thus creating an arms race that precipitates a war. In practice, the realists often advocate creating a superpower that keeps peace, while their opponents advocate a balance of power among equals (Kriesberg 1998, 137, 171).

Our theory may shed some light on the controversy. It suggests that, as the realists argue, nations with overwhelming power indeed can maintain peace. After all, the Romans did it and the United States seems to be doing it. But there are at least two difficulties. First, attempts to achieve such supremacy usually proceed in *small* increments – and that provokes reciprocation, an arms race, and ultimately threatens peace. Second, when the superpower is forced to actually *use* extreme force, it provokes hostility, empowers the opposition, and ultimately endangers peace. Thus we may conclude that, when unusual circumstances have already thrust a nation into the position of an unchallenged superpower, that superpower may help to keep peace – for a while. But when a nation disturbs an existing balance of power by trying to *achieve* superpower status, it endangers – rather than promotes – peace.

### Hostility-Driven Escalation

As you just saw, the fact that a conflict involves two (or more) interacting participants compelled us to distinguish between two aspects of a Party's escalation, unilateral and reciprocated. Equally compelling is another distinction, between conflicts driven by goal incompatibility and those driven by hostility. Because hostility gives conflicts a unique flavor, it merits special consideration.

To begin with, hostility-driven escalation tends to occur for totally trivial reasons, such as a harsh word or unfriendly look. It also tends to be unnecessarily violent, as exemplified when Israelis use live ammunition to disperse a crowd of rock-throwing teenagers, and when Palestinians retaliate by exploding bombs on crowded streets of Israeli towns. Finally, escalation and deescalation may occur with surprising suddenness, such as when riot police quickly disperse demonstrators with water cannons and tear gas.

Moreover, hostility springs from different sources than goal incompatibility: whereas goal incompatibility stems from contests over resources or incompatible roles or values (Figure 3.2), hostility is caused primarily by grievances and frustration (Figure 5.2). Some grievances might be very old, such as when a Serb hates all Muslims because of the fifteenth-century Turkish victory over Serbs.

## A Model of Escalation

You may agree with the main point made so far, that Party's escalation is driven by three forces: its own interests, acts of its Opponent, and its hostility. You may also readily agree to the next point, that escalation will slow down, stop, and eventually turn into deescalation if these forces undergo certain changes: if Party starts deescalating, if Opponent starts deescalating, if hatred is replaced by friendship.

Yet for certain important questions our discussion does not provide a ready answer. Can escalation stop even when these three basic forces do not change? What will happen if Party continues escalating even though Opponent is ready to deescalate? Can lasting peace be obtained without establishing a friendly relationship between former foes? A formal model of conflict can provide the answers.

### Basic Equations

The model consists of the following two equations:

$$dP/dt = rO - uP + h$$
$$r, u > 0 \qquad (7.1)$$
$$dO/dt = rP - uO + h$$

To a mathematician, these equations are simple. Although they may send you into shock, there is a simple cure for that: read each equation as if it stated *the very same ideas as we just expressed in plain English* – that is, correlate English expressions with the symbols in the equation. Observe that, to make this easier, we use symbols that correspond to the *first* letter of the English expression: P is used for *P*arty, O for *O*pponent, and so on. Some of the important "translations" follow:

1. Instead of speaking of "escalation," the equation "says" $dP/dt$.
2. Instead of speaking about "unilateral deescalation," the equation uses $-uP$.[2]
3. Instead of speaking about "reciprocated escalation," it uses $rO$.[3]
4. Instead of "hostility," it uses $h$.

With these interpretations in mind, you can see that the first equation in equations 7.1 says that *Party's escalation (dP/t) depends on its readiness to reciprocate Opponent's escalation (rO), on its readiness to de-escalate unilaterally (−uP), and on its hostility toward its opponent (h).* The second equation says the very same thing about the other side, the Opponent.

You gain further insights when you realize that the equations' right-hand side refers to certain "inner" tendencies, what the actors *contemplate* doing, and the left-hand side to what the actors *actually do.* The actors are portrayed as influenced by three distinct impulses: to retaliate, to escalate, and to express hostility. What they actually do – how much they actually escalate – is a compromise between these three impulses. Technically, the compromise is reached by *adding* the three impulses together. If you keep this point in mind, you will see that it is perfectly possible for Party to wish to escalate and yet act in a deescalatory manner.

Still, several puzzles remain. One of these concerns the symbols "inside" the expressions such as $rO$: do $r$ and $O$ have meaning of their own? They do. The following list – again, for simplicity's sake, focusing on the Party – might provide some answers:

$P$: coerciveness of Party's action.

$O$: coerciveness of Opponent's action.

$dP/dt$: escalation in Party's coerciveness.[4]

$r$: extent to which Party wishes to reciprocate.[5]

$u$: extent to which Party wishes to act *unilaterally*.

$h$: extent to which Party wishes to express hostility.[6]

$rO$: Party's reciprocation.

$uP$: Party's unilateral escalation.

This list suggests that there *is* a conceptual distinction between terms such as $r$ and $O$. The term $r$ corresponds to the extent to which Party reciprocates throughout the conflict, $O$ corresponds to Opponent's coerciveness. You may think of $r$ as an "internal" *tendency* or *disposition* that "normally" does not change because it is "ingrained" in the actor's personality or culture.[7] Such terms are called "parameters." Term $O$ refers to actual *behavior*, to the level of coerciveness used by the Opponent. Because Opponent's coerciveness can – and usually does – change, it is called a "variable."

You may also wonder why the three terms on the right-hand side are *added* together. Why are they not multiplied? The answer is that these equations are nearly identical to those used by Richardson (1960) to determine the conditions under which an arms race could be contained. Being familiar with various models of physical systems with feedbacks,[8] he chose one of the simplest – the equations 7.1.[9] We might add that, to make our discussion of the model as simple as possible, a very special case is considered here: the adversaries are assumed to have the *same* parameters $r$, $u$, and $h$.

Finally, you may wonder why we use $-u$P instead of $+u$P. The reason is purely technical.[10] Unfortunately, the term, $-u$P can be confusing. But this confusion can be relieved if you remember two points. (1) In general, the parameter $u$ stands for the extent to which Party acts unilaterally. (2) When we assume that $u$ is a positive number, the expression $-u$P signifies that Party contemplates *de*escalation; when we assume that $u$ is a negative number, the expression $-u$P specifies that Party contemplates escalation.

### Contributions of the Model

Remember that we promised earlier that a formal model would help us answer three important questions. Can escalation stop even when the "inner" predispositions ($r$, $u$, and $h$) do *not* change? What will happen if only *one* opponent stops escalating? Can lasting peace be obtained without establishing a *friendly* relationship between former foes?

To answer the first question, we must for a moment go back to Richardson's analysis. By examining the implications of the equations 7.1, Richardson showed that the complex give-and-take of escalation has a fairly simple endpoint: usually, Party's coercivenes *converges toward an equilibrium.*[11] More precisely, if (and only if) it is true that

$$h > 0 \text{ and } u > r, \qquad (7.2)$$

then the process will approach an equilibrium state given by Party's coerciveness P* and Opponent's coerciveness O* as:

$$P^* = O^* = \frac{h}{u - r} \qquad (7.3)$$

In plain English: if two similar[12] adversaries are hostile toward each other but are more intent on curbing escalation than on retaliating (the equations 7.2), then their coerciveness will approach the level given by equation 7.3, and, once reaching it, will stay at that level.

Furthermore, it can be shown that *Party will escalate if its first conflict action falls below its equilibrium point.* For example, suppose that two boys have been competing in a schoolyard, getting increasingly irritated with each other. Finally, open fighting breaks out as one of the boys yells that the other is cheating. Considering how hostile the boy feels and how much he wants to win, this action is fairly mild, much less than what it is bound to become. (Translation: the first conflict action is below the equilibrium point.) The other boy responds by calling the first boy a "creep"; the first boy responds by hitting him; the second boy hits back even harder; and so on. Ultimately, they are fighting steadily, exchanging blows whose severity is determined by their anger and will to win the contest. It stays at that level for a while. (Translation: they reached the equilibrium point and are remaining at it.) Of course, they will not fight indefinitely: either they become exhausted, one of them gives up, or the teacher breaks up the fight. (These are deescalation processes, to be considered shortly.)

We are now ready to answer the first question: even when Party's "inner" tendencies (specified by parameters $r$, $u$, and $h$) remain unchanged, its overt behavior can change dramatically, going from escalation to a steady – equilibrium – level of coerciveness. This will happen if (1) Party is hostile toward Opponent (if $h$ is positive), if (2) it is more intent on curbing escalation than on retaliating (if $u > r$),[13] and if (3) Party starts *below* the equilibrium level of coerciveness (see equation 7.3).

A visual illustration might be helpful at this point. Suppose that the two adversaries' parameters ($r$, $u$, and $h$) are identical and that, although they are hostile to each other ($h > 0$), they prefer deescalation to retaliation ($u > r$) – thus satisfying condition 7.2. We chose parameters that meet these assumptions and, although somewhat arbitrary, are fairly realistic:

$$dP/dt = .3Y - .8P + 5$$
$$dY/dt = .3P - .8Y + 5 \tag{7.4}$$

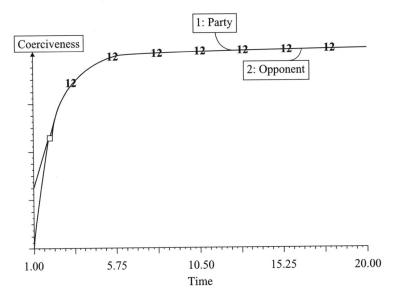

**Figure 7.1.** Escalating toward an Equilibrium

Moreover, to make our illustration more informative, we assumed that Party starts being more aggressive than Opponent.

Using these equations in a computer simulation, we obtained a picture shown in Figure 7.1. Note that, because the inequalities in (7.2) are satisfied, both actors' coerciveness converges toward equilibrium; because both start below the equilibrium, their coerciveness escalates until the equilibrium level is reached; because they have the same parameters, they reach the same equilibrium. Note that *the fact that they start at a different level of coerciveness does not matter* – the equilibrium level depends only on the three parameters.

The second question was, What will happen if Party continues escalation even though Opponent is ready to deescalate? To answer this question, we ran another computer simulation. We again used equations 7.4 but with one modification: we made Party quarrelsome by setting its unilateral deescalation parameter to $u = -1$. The results are shown in Figure 7.2: as expected, Party continues its nonstop escalation; but – and this may come as a surprise – Opponent engages in nonstop escalation as well, in spite of his conciliatory intentions!

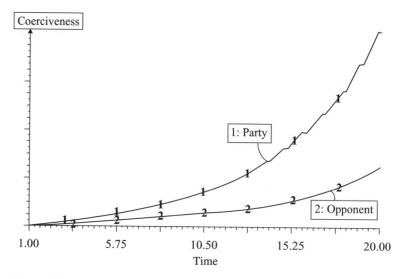

**Figure 7.2.** Party's Strong Tendency to Escalate Causes Opponent to Escalate
As Well

We now can answer the second question: as long as Party is on the
path of ever increasing escalation, Opponent will follow suit even when
he does not want to. This discrepancy between his intentions and his
actual behavior occurs because, once Party is locked in an uncompro-
mising stance, once its parameters guarantee never-ending escalation,
Opponent's tendency to reciprocate ($r$P) is sufficient to pull him into
what he does not wish to do, resulting in a runaway escalation.

The third question our model was supposed to answer was, Can
stable peace be obtained without establishing a friendly relationship
between former foes? If we understand by "stable peace" a condition
of zero coerciveness,[14] then the answer is, No, lasting peace can be
obtained only when all hostilities disappear. This is because the only
way of achieving an equilibrium of $P^* = O^* = 0$ is when $h = 0$.[15]

### The Model and the Real World

Rapoport ([1960] 1961, 37) shows that the equations 7.1 do a fairly
good job of predicting what Richardson intended them to predict – an
arms race. But when they are used to do what they were *not* designed

to do – to describe *general* conflict behavior – do they perform equally well? The answer seems to be that they do, provided we change some of the assumptions we made in equations 7.1.

We may start by considering the assumption about the first parameter, the reciprocation parameter $r$. Were we justified assuming that the actors will always try to reciprocate ($r > 0$)? Recall that we argued that, although the tendency to retaliate (and, more generally, to reciprocate) can be "outvoted" by rational considerations, it can never be *extinguished*. This means that our original assumption was correct, that actors will always reciprocate (that $r$ will always be a positive number).

But the assumption that actors will always try to *de*escalate the conflict (that $u > 0$) is a different story. We have argued that under certain conditions actors may in fact *escalate* so heavily that their tendency to act unilaterally must be escalatory (that parameter $u$ must be negative). This can happen when an aggressor, wanting to win quickly, uses all the force he or she can muster; when a nation has overwhelming power; or when an actor has a belligerent personality or culture. Thus we must allow that the unilateral action parameter $u$ be not only positive but negative as well.

But we must recognize that if the conflict lasts long enough, actors with a tendency to escalate unilaterally ($u < 0$) are bound to reverse themselves. Sooner or later, a feedback will occur that forces them to halt escalation and, ultimately, to start unilateral *de*escalation ($u > 0$) – if for no other reason than because they have reached the end of their resources. (See the discussion of feedbacks given later in this chapter.)

### Escalation Due to "Original" Conditions

Because much of the early escalation in a conflict is due to the same main conditions that led to the start of open conflict actions, the theory of Chapter 5 helps us to understand not only why conflicts become open but also why they escalate. In particular, high conflict solidarity and abundant conflict resources – the main reasons for the start of open conflicts (see Figure 5.2) – determine how much Party will escalate unilaterally, how strongly it will reciprocate Opponent's conflict actions, and how hostile it will feel toward him. For example, the warlike culture of the Apaches – an important component of their conflict solidarity – would not only cause them to attack another tribe; it would also induce them to escalate violence once a conflict was on its way: they might kill those who opposed them as well as those who did not, and they might burn the entire village.

## Escalation Due to Changing Conditions

Some conflicts last for a long time. For example, Israel and Syria have maintained a sporadic conflict for decades. Syria did it by proxy, by supporting radical movements that made sporadic attacks on Israel; Israel did it more directly, by attacking suspected enemy bases with retaliatory air strikes. But many conflicts, after remaining in an equilibrium for a while, begin either to escalate or to deescalate. Technically, this means that in these conflicts some of the model's parameters ($r$, $u$, or $h$) have changed.

To see what happens when even one of the parameters is changed, let us rerun the simulation that yielded Figure 7.2. As in that figure, Opponent favors deescalation while Party is bent on escalation ($u = -.1$). But the situation soon changes: at time t $= 10$ Party starts favoring strong unilateral *de*escalation ($u = +.9$). True, this is a drastic change, but such changes can occur in the real world. For example, Party might have suffered a crushing defeat that destroyed its resources and demoralized its troops. In any case, as Figure 7.3 shows, the consequences of

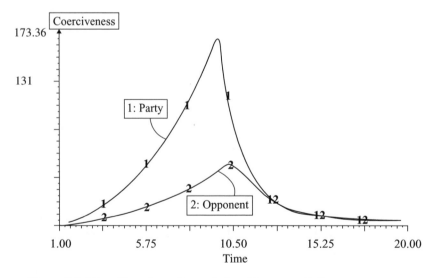

**Figure 7.3.** When Party Starts Deescalating, Opponent Follows

this parameter shift are startling: at $t = 10$, Party (whose behavior is represented by line 1) begins deescalating rapidly, continuing to do so until it reaches an equilibrium of low coerciveness. Because we chose the final parameters of the two sides to be the same, Opponent and Party ultimately reach the same equilibrium.

Why then do adversaries ever go above the equilibrium levels of co-erciveness, becoming more willing to escalate unilaterally, more bent on revenge, or more hostile? Some of the causes are external to the conflict itself. For example, one of the conflict groups may gain new allies and thus become more powerful. But by far the most common reason is that the feedbacks from the conflict transform the adversaries themselves.

### Feedbacks That Increase Escalation

As the conflict progresses, it unleashes certain processes that mag-nify the propensities that govern escalation: the propensity to escalate unilaterally, to retaliate, or to be hostile. Some of these changes occur because of events that strengthen Party's solidarity.

*Increase in Conflict Solidarity.* Some theories and research suggest that conflict solidarity can increase because *individual perceptions* have changed. As Kriesberg (1998, 152–154) notes, this happens when in-dividual members strive to resolve their "cognitive dissonance" by justifying the violence of their actions; when they start to "perceive selectively," ignoring their own excesses and exaggerating those of the opponents; and when, being "entrapped" by having invested heavily in the conflict, they begin to protect their investments. Be-cause making these changes is not easy, they seek advice and rein-forcement from fellow members of the group, so free interaction increases. This interaction ultimately results in a new, more radical ideology and greater conflict solidarity. As an example of how these processes can change individual perceptions, recall that, in the not-so-distant past, some presumably law-abiding Americans took part in lynching – an action that was not only illegal but normally morally repugnant.

*Opponent's* coercive behavior also tends to strengthen conflict sol-idarity. This is particularly true when the Opponent commits brutal acts, as when police beat up demonstrators or when the military executes innocent civilians. Such acts cause the members of the aggrieved group to see the opponents as subhuman and evil and create a desire for revenge.

A long-lasting conflict can also increase conflict solidarity by making the goals of the conflict groups more *incompatible*. This may occur when radical groups – such as minorities or special interest groups – join in the conflict, and their goals are added to the agenda. For example, an early conflict between the timber industry and the U.S. Forest Service was about areas in which trees might be cut. When environmentalists joined the fight, the industry's right to cut any trees at all was questioned. Another possibility is that, as conflict proceeds, minor issues may gain symbolic importance (Kriesberg 1998, 158–159). For example, the proposed regulation of hand guns may come to symbolize a threat to a constitutional right to bear arms.

As conflict progresses, certain *structural* changes may occur. The original leaders may become more radical; radical leaders may emerge as marginal groups join the struggle; specialists in violence, such as police and the military, may be brought in to direct conflict behavior. All this tends to promote further escalation.

*Increase in Conflict Resources.* So far, we have been discussing feedbacks that affect conflict solidarity and some processes related to it. But Party's changes in conflict resources can play an equally important role: if they increase, unilateral escalation often results. Thus a wife who has been unhappy with her marriage may decide to file for divorce when she becomes financially independent; nations at war may capture weapons or territory that increase its capacity to escalate the conflict.

*Strategic Escalation.* We need to account for a seemingly paradoxical fact: Party often escalates when it is in danger of becoming *weaker*. For example, a husband who has been fighting with his wife discovers that she is contemplating a divorce. To avoid heavy payments in case a divorce occurs, he starts divesting himself of many of his funds (an escalatory action). A general, on learning that the opposing army is planning an attack, may forestall it by launching an attack of his own. To account for this paradox, we need a new concept, one that takes into account the fact that adversaries engage in *strategic* deliberations – the concept of "strategic escalation." Thus, when threatened, Party may make a preemptive strike because to do so is to its strategic advantage (because to do so is "rational").

There are other situations that make strategic escalation advisable. Some of them are "internal." For example, when members grow dissatisfied with the conflict, leaders may escalate in hopes that Opponent's response will infuriate their (Party's) members and thus increase their conflict solidarity.

## Deescalation Due to Changing Conditions

After a conflict has been in an equilibrium for a long time, it tends to deescalate. Again, some of the reasons may be external to the conflict itself. For example, when NATO forces entered the Kosovo conflict, Serbian forces began to withdraw. But there are internal reasons as well, mainly the feedbacks from the conflict itself. Let us consider how a change in action propensities may start a chain of deescalation.

### Process of Deescalation

Our model suggests that a stalemated conflict will start deescalating only if the equilibrium level of coerciveness ($P^*$ and $O^*$) becomes *lower*. And the equilibrium equation 7.3,

$$P^* = O^* = \frac{h}{u - r},$$

suggests that this can occur for three main reasons: hostility ($h$) can decrease, the tendency to deescalate ($u$) can increase, or the tendency to retaliate ($r$) can become smaller.

Thus the stalemated conflict between the United States and Iraq can start deescalating when the adversaries begin to be less *hostile* toward each other (when their $h$ decreases). For example, the media in both countries may start depicting the opponent in less negative terms. Deescalation can also start when both sides start deescalating *unilaterally* more vigorously (when their $u$ increases). For example, the United States can start diminishing its flights over Iraqi territory. Or deescalation can start when the adversaries become less eager to *retaliate* (when $r$ becomes smaller). For example, the United States may decide not to tighten its embargo against Iraq when the latter refuses to admit weapons inspectors to its military facilities.

The equations 7.1 suggest that, in order for deescalation to continue, some of the three propensities ($h$, $u$, and $r$) *must continue to change* in a manner that promotes deescalation. Thus the United States and Iraq must become increasingly less hostile, or more intent on curbing escalation, or less retaliatory. This approach makes sense intuitively: if all three propensities remained the same while coerciveness was decreasing, deescalation would soon stop at the level appropriate to those propensities. But it is possible to prove this conclusion more rigorously.[16]

Finally, the model suggests that deescalation will eliminate *all* coerciveness (that P* and O* will become zero) only if all hostile feelings stop (only if $h$ becomes zero).[17] Thus for the United States and Iraq to stop all coercive interactions, their media may have to stop attacking the other side altogether.

### Feedbacks That Lead to Deescalation

As a struggle continues for a long time, forces may be unleashed that lead to deescalation. Not suprisingly, they affect the main bases of conflict action: conflict solidarity and conflict resources.

*Decrease in Conflict Solidarity.* As a war drags on, many individuals become impoverished, possibly losing members of their families. At the same time, the wealthy and the powerful may profit from the conflict, thus increasing social *inequality* and popular dissatisfaction with the conflict. Military desertions and public demonstrations opposing the conflict may occur with increasing frequency (Kriesberg 1998, 185).

Dissatisfaction and disillusionment that lower conflict solidarity may bring about *organizational* changes. New leaders may emerge, opposing the policies of the hard-liners, and advocating accommodation with the enemy. The hard-liners may try to suppress the opposition, but, as we saw earlier, this creates hostility toward them and ultimately strengthens the opposition. For example, when, in the 1990s, the moderate South African government freed Nelson Mandela, the leader of the African National Congress (ANC), conservative white opposition to the government grew, and in 1993 members of that opposition assassinated a major figure in the ANC. This murder galvanized the moderates into action: the ANC organized protest demonstrations and the government arrested a member of the Conservative Party in connection with the murder (Kriesberg 1998, 208).

*Depletion of Conflict Resources.* A long conflict also depletes adversaries' conflict resources. The most obvious reason is that there are *natural limits* on most conflict resources. For example, a labor union has only limited funds to support the strikers; a nation has only a limited supply of manpower and strategic materials such as oil; boys have only limited strength they can apply against each other.

Another reason is that the conflict actions of the adversaries usually *destroy or disable* each other's "assets": in a war, soldiers are killed, ships are sunk, airplanes are shot down; during a strike, some of the strikers may be arrested and put in jail; during a schoolyard fight, the boys may hurt each other. Wartime destruction not only hampers the efforts of the fighting forces but also causes shortages of food and disruption of services, thus weakening conflict solidarity. But even nonmilitary conflicts can lead to frustrating deprivations. When a union goes on strike, the workers lose their pay and the company loses profits; when husband and wife fight, they deprive each other of needed love and support.

*Strategic Deescalation.* Depletion of conflict resources may do more than hinder aggressive action, it may suggest that a fundamental reassessment of conflict strategy is in order. After careful deliberation, Party may decide that, even though it has sufficient resources to continue the struggle, the future looks bleak, and it may therefore decide to sue for peace. Results may range from a total surrender that gives the Opponent all or most of his goals to an accommodation in which both sides reach some of their goals.

*Ending the Conflict.* Our earlier discussion notwithstanding,[18] in the real world the adversaries need *not* have the same levels of equilibrium coerciveness. The adversary with more resources and greater conflict solidarity will be able to sustain a higher level of coerciveness, thus gradually wearing its opponent down. For example, when NATO became involved in the Kosovo conflict, the Serbs, being the weaker party, were more eager to curb their coerciveness and less willing (and able) to retaliate than were the NATO forces. Consequently, when that conflict reached a stalemate, with NATO maintaining constant bombing of Serb targets, the Serb position was gradually eroded. Finally, the Serbs agreed to pull out of Kosovo, thus handing NATO what appeared to be nearly complete victory, albeit at considerable human and economic cost. Although the role of that bombing remains controversial,[19] our theory suggests that this show of overwhelming force made it rational for Serbs to deescalate.

Of course, one can prevail by means other than wearing down the opponent. In many cases, it suffices for one of the adversaries suddenly to become much stronger. This was the case when the United States developed an atomic bomb and dropped it on Japan. Although Japan's forces were depleted by then and an end of war was in sight, Japan probably capitulated earlier than it would have otherwise.[20]

But however the conflict ends, what matters most is what happens *afterward*. Are the surrender terms so harsh that the defeated adversary cannot live with them? When the Versailles treaty imposed humiliating terms on Germany, the "victors" created conditions for a new, more deadly conflict – World War II.

Ancient warriors were quite aware of this problem and had a cruel "solution": they often killed most of the defeated adversaries and burned their towns to the ground. Fortunately, this strategy is impossible today, so another approach is needed: the victors must be generous, making it possible for the vanquished to live well. It is not coincidental that victors in a sporting event heap praises on the defeated opponent. Nor was it accidental that, some time after the Germans were defeated in World War II, the United States offered them economic help through the Marshall Plan. Although some scholars question U.S. motivation, pointing out that this plan was very profitable for American business, it is clear that it helped Germany reach prosperity.

*Accommodation.* The second – and usually the best – way to end a conflict is through an accommodation, an agreement that is acceptable to both sides. The effectiveness of processes such as negotiation, mediation, and arbitration has been well established (see Chapter 9).

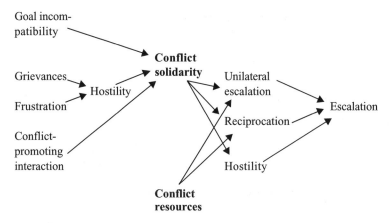

**Figure 7.4.** Original Causes That Contribute to Escalation

## Conclusions

One of the fundamental insights into escalation (and deescalation) is that it may be driven by the very same causes that led to the outbreak of hostilities in the first place. Figure 7.4 expresses this insight graphically. Note that this diagram is essentially the same as that given in Figure 5.2: conflict solidarity and conflict resources again play a crucial role. The main difference is that Figure 7.4 adds the three "forces" that drive escalation: unilateral action $(-\text{uP})$, reciprocation $(r\text{O})$, and hostility $(h)$.

Although Figure 7.4 is largely self-explanatory, a clarification may be helpful. Note that "hostility" appears twice, once as a cause of conflict solidarity (original hostility), and once as a *consequence* of solidarity (subsequent hostility). This is meant to suggest that the process that increases conflict solidarity also tends to increase hostility toward Opponent.

Although escalation can occur even when the original conditions do not change, typically they *do* change. Theoretically most interesting are the changes caused by the conflict itself, by its "feedbacks." Figure 7.5 shows the most important escalatory feedbacks. It shows that some feedbacks increase conflict *solidarity.* As reports of the opponents' brutality come in, members of the conflict group become increasingly angry; as radical groups begin to participate in the conflict, and as

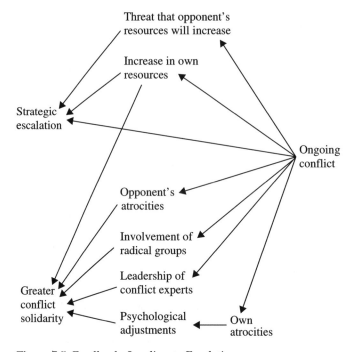

**Figure 7.5.** Feedbacks Leading to Escalation

coerciveness experts move into leadership positions, the group's ideology becomes more radical; as it becomes obvious that "our side" is committing brutal acts as well, members undergo psychological changes that justify their actions and increase their participation. Other feedbacks, such as their side's victory, may increase their *resources*.

Ongoing conflict may also create conditions that call for *strategic* escalation: if Party is threatened with an increase in Opponent's resources, it may be wise for it to make a preemptive strike; if its resources are significantly increased, then it may escalate in hopes of prevailing. Note that one arrow in Figure 7.5 leads directly from "ongoing conflict" to "strategic escalation": this indicates that there may be other feedbacks (not considered here) that invite strategic reassessment.

But a conflict can also create feedbacks that lead to deescalation. As Figure 7.6 shows, when the conflict has lasted for a long time, it generates feedbacks that decrease both conflict solidarity and conflict

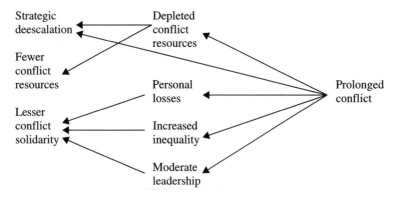

**Figure 7.6.** Feedbacks Leading to Deescalation

resources. Conflict *solidarity* may decrease because many are losing wealth or family members; because profiteering increases economic inequality; because, as fatigue spreads, moderate leaders gain power. Moreover, as conflict continues, conflict *resources* get depleted. This affects Party's coerciveness in two ways: it decreases Party's ability to engage in coercive action and thus forces unilateral deescalation;[21] and it calls for strategic reassessment that might suggest even more drastic deescalation.

Not all conflicts end through gradual deescalation; some end in sudden one-sided defeat. The old wisdom that one can win the war but lose the peace is very pertinent here. Unless the "victors" are generous and allow the defeated adversary to live well and with dignity, they will have created conditions favoring a new conflict – one that they may not win.

In the next chapter we shall apply our escalation theory to the Bosnian civil war. But first, it may be helpful to revisit the civil rights conflict to see how our theory could account for its escalation.

## The Civil Rights Struggle Revisited

If we review the historical path of the sit-ins in the civil rights struggle, we can see clearly how the "root" causes, working through intermediate causes, moved the activists and their opponents toward escalation. Of course, not all the conditions need be present to the same degree for escalation to occur. The ideological tenets of racial equality and nonviolent resistance to evil led the civil rights advocates to some acts of unilateral escalation. Ideology also gave them a long-term perspective requiring that they stand firm, even if that firmness was perceived by their segregationist opponents as retaliation. Clear value incompatibility between protesters and southern white society produced high levels of black resentment, or what one may call restrained hostility. The frustration over the slow pace of integration and an increased sense of the injustice caused by unequal treatment combined to raise protester hostility levels. A mood of challenge, readiness to push further, and increasingly hostile feelings combined to move the sit-in protesters to escalate the conflict.

It would be difficult to imagine less compatible sets of values than those that confronted one another in the South during the sit-ins. Racial integration and racial segregation were diametrically opposed concepts and practices. A majority of southern whites believed in racial inequality and separation. That such a deeply rooted belief and practice, indeed an entire way of life, was being called into question was deeply disturbing to most whites. A high level of frustration and anxiety was thereby produced among them.

Then there were the injustices and grievances perceived by the defenders of segregation. For a century, as they saw it, during the Civil War and after, the Union side had imposed its power and prejudice upon the South. The resentment of the loser was still very much present. With the racial integration the North was imposing its culture and racial etiquette as well. These factors combined to produce high levels of hostility, belligerence, and readiness to retaliate among southern whites. Thus the potential for escalation was high, and it did indeed occur over long periods and in many racial settings during the 1960s.

Escalation was also fueled by increasing solidarity. In the sit-in movement, the African American students had many northern supporters and a high level of solidarity to give them substantial if not overwhelming power. The conviction of moral rightness was an additional source of their strength.[22] These conditions raised their readiness to be coercive through physical intervention in the places that denied them service by custom and law. Their confidence also grew that they could successfully retaliate against their opponents' resistance.

Their opponents, the white segregationists, were likewise persuaded toward escalation. Like the protesters, they felt that moral authority ("separate is right"), backed by southern law and custom, was on their side. Racial solidarity (despite obvious class differences) among whites empowered them. They had most of the wealth, all of the police power, and a major part of the organizational know-how to serve their resistance to this challenge by blacks. And they certainly had a belligerent ideology – combining southern military tradition, vigilante violence, and racial hatred. These factors heightened their readiness to escalate and to suppress the open challenge to Southern racial power distribution that civil rights activism represented.

# CHAPTER EIGHT

# Application to Conflict in Bosnia

IN THE PRECEDING CHAPTER, we suggested how conflict, once it has emerged, can intensify through escalation. We saw how various factors can make conflict parties more hostile, more retaliatory, and less willing to curb coerciveness, thus leading to escalation. There is hardly a better contemporary real-world illustration of this process than the Bosnian civil war of the 1990s. In this chapter, we apply our theory of escalation to that case. We thereby add a cross-national illustration to the intraorganizational and intrasocietal cases used in earlier chapters.

## The Bosnian Conflict

The origins of the Bosnian conflict are more complex than we have space to explore here. However, we do present an account of its post–World War II roots for the reader in the Appendix, "Prelude to the Dissolution of Yugoslavia."[1] Here we present only the historical background immediately preceding the escalation of the conflict, the central concern of the chapter.

As the Bosnian civil war developed from 1991 to 1995, four main conflict groups were involved. Group 1 comprised the government of the Republic of Croatia (Zagreb) and the Croat minority in Bosnia. When those two acted together, as was usually the case, we refer to them as "Croats." Group 2, the government of the Bosnian republic and its forces, was very much a multiethnic body in 1991 but by 1995 had become mostly Muslim. We refer to this group as the "Bosnian government," because an independent, multiethnic Bosnia was its intention. Group 3, the Federal Republic of Yugoslavia (Serbia-Montenegro) and the Republika Serbska set up by the Serb minority in Bosnia, we call "Greater Serbs" when the two subgroups acted together, because a Greater Serbia was their motivating dream, although as the war progressed the Bosnian Serbs acted more and more independently of Belgrade. Group 4 was a collection of international organizations from outside the region: the United Nations (UN), the North Atlantic Treaty Organization (NATO), the Contact Group (CG), and the European Union (EU). We refer to them by their respective names or acronyms.

For the reader's convenience, Figure 8.1 shows a recent map of the former Yugoslavia (as adapted from the *New York Times*, 2001). Within Bosnia, Croats, Serbs, and Muslims have come to occupy different regions as a consequence of the population dislocations occurring during the civil war.

The escalation of conflict in Bosnia was the last step in the rapid series of secessions of republics from the former Yugolavia occurring in 1991. Two secessions were relatively peaceful: Slovenia's withdrawal was only moderately contested by Belgrade, because few Serbs lived there, and Macedonia was protected by a United Nations preventive deployment force. But the secession of Croatia, home to a large Serb minority, left many thousands of Serbs under the control of non-Serbs and led to civil war. It made Bosnian independence more likely to be violently resisted.

Slovenian and Croatian nationalism had confirmed and stimulated Greater Serbian nationalism. For some time, the Serbs throughout Yugoslavia had seen themselves increasingly at risk of being overwhelmed by the other ethnic nationalities. How they perceived the demographic shifts taking place since World War II influenced heavily their sense of identity and insecurity. While the Bosnian conflict appeared to most of the world as Serb aggression, Serbs saw it very differently. Between 1879 and 1991, they had watched their proportion in Bosnia's population shrink (from 43 to 31 percent), while Muslims increased theirs (from 39 to 44 percent).[2] It was not difficult to convince

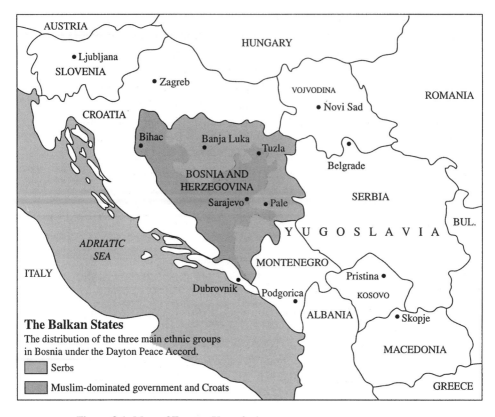

**Figure 8.1.** Map of Former Yugoslavia

most Bosnian Serbs that Bosnia's declaration of independence confirmed their increasingly minority status.

This Serbian sense of losing ground in the former Yugoslavia, in
both numbers and influence, fed easily into the Serbs' historical
identity as victims, beginning with their fifteenth-century defeats by
the Turks. Although Tito's federal Yugoslavia had held that grievance
at bay, its rapid collapse in 1991 delivered Serb fears and resentments
to political and military leaders who exploited them fully for personal
political ends. The aggressive action of the Greater Serbs in Bosnia

(and later in Kosovo) was, in their view, only the latest episode in a centuries-long resistance to oppression.

### Conflict around and within Bosnia

The Bosnian civil war was a late episode in the disintegration of the former Yugoslavia. Although it was a discrete conflict with its own internal dynamics of escalation and deescalation, it cannot be understood apart from the earlier episodes, particularly what was going on along and through its borders with Croatia and the Federal Republic (Serbia-Montenegro). The Bosnian conflict was structured by the Croatian war immediately preceding it. In that war, the largely Serbian "Krajina" region of Croatia had declared itself an autonomous region. The Croatian government moved to reassert its control there, and the Yugoslav People's Army intervened in support of Croatian Serbs. Although Bosnia tried to stay out of the war, both Croatia and the Federal Republic increasingly treated contiguous areas of Bosnia as their own territory, arming their coreligionists there and otherwise undermining Bosnia's integrity and independence.

Once the bonds of the former Yugoslavia had been broken, the new power centers in the capitals of the Federal Republic (Belgrade) and Croatia (Zagreb) promptly set about mobilizing the resources needed to build the envisioned Greater Serbia and Greater Croatia their leaders were promoting. The Serb minorities in Croatia and Bosnia were to be assisted in every way by the Greater Serb leaders to formalize their ethnic and religious ties and aspirations with their "motherland." In Croatia, the sentiment for bringing the Croat minorities and territories in Bosnia under the protection and control of their "motherland" was growing. But as late as the early spring of 1992, Bosnian Croats were still voting overwhelmingly for and as a part of an independent Bosnia.

When in June 1991 Croatia declared its independence, a war of secession ensued with the Federal Republic. When it ended in January 1992, the Serb-Croat conflict shifted to Bosnian territory, thus drawing in the Bosnian government as a third conflict party. Although both Greater Croats and Greater Serbs were opposing a Bosnian government that was struggling to maintain Bosnia as a multiethnic political and cultural entity, they were also fighting one another. Serbs, Croats, and Muslims in Bosnia, who since World War II had increasingly lived side by side, sometimes intermarried, and generally lived in peace with one another as Yugoslavs, would quickly slip into internecine conflict.

While ethnic hostility became the facile explanation of the civil war of the popular press, Ignatieff (1997, 46–48) rightly reminds us that it was the collapse of the Yugoslav state that encouraged and permitted the ethnic nationalist violence, not the reverse. Yugoslavs had lived together rather peacefully for more than fifty years. With the fear and paranoia engendered by the rapid collapse of the Yugoslav federation and the proliferation of ethnic military and paramilitary forces, the multiple identities Yugoslavs had grown to live with were no longer possible.

From 1991 onward, the governments of Croatia and the Federal Republic used their considerable communication facilities to reawaken Greater Croat and Greater Serb identities, the memories of historical injustices, and fear of the "other." Those divisive emotions had been muted and largely forgotten in Tito's multicultural Yugoslavia, but they had not completely died out. Once the fear of the "other" was rekindled, only direct violence was needed to justify it and provoke retaliation. Self-serving political and military leaders enabled that violence and cruelty to occur by force of arms. While, under less radical conditions, Bosnia's history of multiethnic coexistence and intercommunal tolerance might have immunized its people against extremism, it could not resist the Greater Serbian and Greater Croatian political and military actions. The conflict, now in the open, escalated inexorably.

### How the Bosnian Conflict Developed

The Bosnian conflict originated, as most conflicts do, in the incompatibility of the goals of the Greater Serbs, Greater Croats, and Muslim Bosnians.[3] That incompatibility lay particularly in resources contested by the three conflict groups and in differing cultural values. For analytical simplification, we discuss here only the Greater Serb–Bosnian government conflict relationship, though the same theoretical explanation holds for the Greater Croat–Bosnian conflict as well, if to a somewhat lesser degree.

The resources contested by the Greater Serbs and Bosnian government were the territory and loyalty of the Serb minority in Bosnia. The Serbs in Bosnia had close historical ties with those in both the Federal Republic and Croatia, and wished to incorporate the territory occupied by them, in some fashion, into "Greater Serbia." The Bosnian government, having declared Bosnian independence in October 1991, wished to preserve that territory and its occupants as a part of its republic.

The Greater Serbs wished to annex Bosnian territory because they believed that the secessionist Bosnian government had no right to govern Bosnian Serbs. They maintained that Bosnia had never been a true state with an independent political tradition, that it was merely Tito's creation designed to violate the rights of Serbs (Rogel 1998, 45). They believed that much of Bosnian territory was rightfully theirs. This belief was fueled by a long history of conquest, from a medieval Serbian state onward, and it romanticized in particular the Serb heroes killed in a battle with the Ottoman Turks in 1389. It saw Serbs from then on as defenders of the Christian faith against the "infidel" Muslims (Rogel 1998, 49). That view called for restoring the glory of the past, by force if necessary.

The cultural values of the Greater Serbs and the Bosnians differed because of certain historical events. Serbs were Slavs, arriving in the Balkans in the seventh century A.D. Although they originally consisted of many independent – and often quarreling – tribes, they achieved a measure of unity in the eighth century, and soon were converted to Orthodox Christianity and the Cyrillic alphabet, preserving that Slavic-Orthodox-Cyrillic heritage to the present day.

The Bosnians, by contrast, had a much weaker cultural identity. Since about 1000 B.C., Bosnia had been occupied by a succession of cultures: first by Illyrians, a people of Indo-European origin; then in the sixth century A.D. by Slavs, who by the seventh century had thoroughly slavonized the area's people. Then, in the fifteenth century, Turkish conquest brought Bosnia into the Ottoman Empire, to remain there until Bosnia's absorption by the Austro-Hungarian Empire in the latter part of the nineteenth century. During Ottoman rule, many Serbs in Bosnia became Muslims, though continuing to speak Serbian.

To coalesce into distinct conflict groups, the Serbs, Croats, and Muslims needed new identities to replace their former ones as citizens of a unified Yugoslavia. Because Serbs were the most widely settled ethnic group throughout Yugoslavia, the Greater Serb propaganda from Belgrade seemed more and more credible in its allegation of a growing threat to Serb minorities. At the same time, Croatians – and, to a lesser degree, Bosnians – encouraged nationalisms of their own, thus confirming the worst fears and suspicions of the Serbs. Those fears were further heightened by international condemnation of Serb militarism, which Serbs saw as one-sided. The Serbian perception of "us against the world" created yet more ethnic solidarity among them.

Conflict solidarity among Greater Serbs was enhanced by Belgrade's promotion of a Serb nationalist ideology heavy with religious symbolism, cultural myths and legend, and revisionist history. It justified their coercive policies against the Bosnian Muslims as historical "score-settling" for the sixteenth-century brutality of Muslim Turks against the Serbs. It appealed to Serbian pride and nationalism by advocating measures such as an increased use of the traditional Cyrillic alphabet, permitting the Orthodox Church to build new and restore old churches (something that was forbidden under socialism), and adopting a militant song as a Greater Serbian national anthem. All of this increased the standing of Serb leader Milosevic among the Greater Serbs (Ramet 1996, 26–27).

These measures served to unify Serbs both in Serbia proper and in Croatia, Bosnia, and the Kosovo region. By contrast, Bosnian "nationalism," as it was of necessity multiethnic, could only emphasize the history of Bosnia as a political and cultural entity over many centuries, and its tradition of ethnic tolerance.

At the same time, various conditions created a high level of frustration. Yugoslavia had slipped into the economic doldrums throughout the 1980s. Inflation, strikes, pay delays, a mounting international debt, collapse of foreign markets for Yugoslav goods, and corruption had all severely reduced the standard of living of the average Croat, Serb, and Bosnian. The frustration was exploited by corrupt ethnic party leaders. Strengthened by the 1974 constitutional revisions and empowered by the 1990 elections, such men had been forging links with mafia-like groups to further expand their power (Kaldor 1999, 37). It thus may be assumed that by 1990 the level of frustration throughout Yugoslavia was high.

Once the elections of 1990 had given them new legitimacy, the leaders of the Federal Republic speedily prepared their political and economic organizations for self-defense and national territorial growth. They consolidated their control in Serbia and Montenegro through purges of their opponents. Meanwhile, the Greater Serbs within Bosnia had been preparing to establish (as they had in Croatia) an "autonomous region" to be aligned with the Federal Republic. Once Bosnia had declared its independence, the ethnic parties there were organized politically for the Greater Serb–Bosnian conflict.

By the time open conflict began in 1992, the Bosnian Serbs had a force of 80,000 supported by units of the Serb-led Yugoslav People's Army (estimated to number about 89,000); the Bosnian government had only a poorly equipped fighting force of about 50,000 (Rogel 1998, 32).

The sparks that ignited the Bosnian conflict were the declaration of Bosnian independence in October 1991 and the referendum to confirm it in February 1992. In April 1992 Bosnian Serbs attacked the forces of the Bosnian government.

### Escalation of the Conflict

Figure 8.2 presents the major events of the conflict from 1991 to 1996, and shows how they escalated and deescalated the level of coerciveness. Although the conflict parties increased and decreased their coercive activity on different schedules (and our theoretical analysis focuses on Greater Serb coerciveness alone), the general coerciveness level, as shown in Figure 8.2, can be said to have risen sharply until early 1994, then climbed more slowly to somewhat of a plateau, with a spike of Serb attacks and NATO responses in mid-1995, and a steady decrease from then on.

Several events strongly affected the course of conflict. The cease-fire that suspended the Croatian war, permitted both Greater Serbs and Greater Croats to turn their full attention to their respective goals in Bosnia. Each continued to establish military and political spheres of activity in the border regions where Croats and Serbs were the majority population. All three conflict groups – Greater Serbs, Greater Croats, and Bosnians – had sovereign governments and armed forces active in Bosnia by March 1992.

Through military offensives and "cleansing" activities, the Greater Serbs by mid-1992 had gained control of perhaps 60 percent of Bosnia, using rape, village destruction, and civilian expulsion as effective

Figure

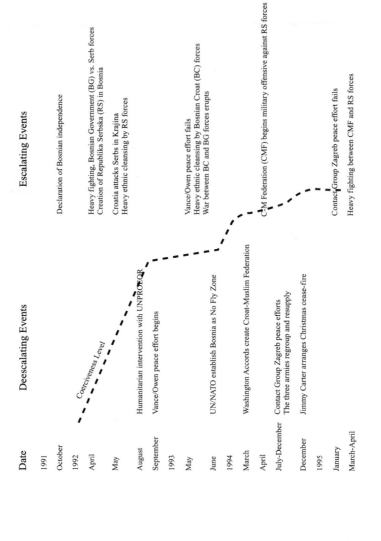

| Date | Deescalating Events | Escalating Events |
|---|---|---|
| 1991 | | |
| October | | Declaration of Bosnian independence |
| 1992 | | |
| April | | Heavy fighting, Bosnian Government (BG) vs. Serb forces / Creation of Republika Serbska (RS) in Bosnia |
| May | | Croatia attacks Serbs in Krajina / Heavy ethnic cleansing by RS forces |
| August | Humanitarian intervention with UNPROFOR | |
| September | Vance/Owen peace effort begins | |
| 1993 | | |
| May | | Vance/Owen peace effort fails / Heavy ethnic cleansing by Bosnian Croat (BC) forces / War between BC and BG forces erupts |
| June | UN/NATO establish Bosnia as No Fly Zone | |
| 1994 | | |
| March | Washington Accords create Croat-Muslim Federation | |
| April | | C-M Federation (CMF) begins military offensive against RS forces |
| July-December | Contact Group Zagreb peace efforts / The three armies regroup and resupply | |
| December | Jimmy Carter arranges Christmas cease-fire | |
| 1995 | | |
| January | | Contact Group Zagreb peace effort fails |
| March-April | | Heavy fighting between CMF and RS forces |

Coerciveness Level

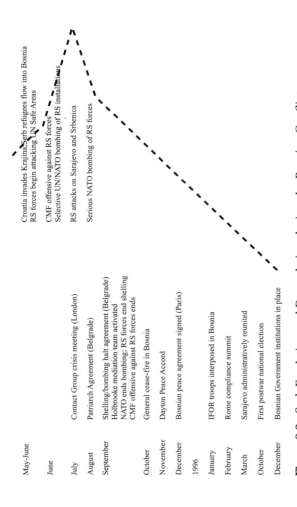

**Figure 8.2.** Serb Escalation and Deescalation during the Bosnian Conflict

weapons of conquest. By 1993 Greater Croat and Bosnian government forces had improved and were engaging Greater Serb forces and especially one another with increasing frequency. Violence against civilian populations was used by all sides. In 1994 a shaky Croat-Muslim Federation was cobbled together that reduced Croat-Muslim coerciveness but increased military activity by the two against Greater Serbs. By 1995, international organizations were intervening increasingly against the Greater Serbs, who retaliated with growing force against UN/NATO safe areas and forces.

## Moderating Efforts

Moderating efforts, particularly by the physical presence of international organizations, had various effects at different times on the degree of coerciveness used in the conflict. The presence of the International Red Cross, for example, did appear to have a moderating influence because the most brutal five weeks of the war immediately followed its withdrawal in May 1992 (Ignatieff 1997, 133).

When, in August 1992, the United Nations dispatched a humanitarian intervention force of seven thousand to Bosnia to provide food and shelter for the refugees from ethnic cleansing and military action, fighting appeared to moderate temporarily. In the long run, however, this intervention actually escalated the conflict as Bosnian Serbs (and occasionally Bosnian government forces) seized UN weapons containment depots and refugee centers and held UN troops hostage.

Later UN and European Union peace efforts had similarly ambiguous consequences. In September 1992 Cyrus Vance and David Lord Owen began an eight-month mediation process, which did provide a temporary negotiating forum while fighting continued. By early 1993 this effort had produced the elements of settlement through much consultation with and involvement of the Bosnians themselves – Croats, Serbs, and the Bosnian government (Owen 1995).

When the Vance-Owen effort collapsed in May 1993, serious fighting erupted between Greater Croat and Bosnian government forces. Throughout May and June, heavy ethnic cleansing went on as Greater Croats expanded their territory. The UN and NATO implemented a "no fly zone" throughout Bosnia, attempting to moderate the fighting by limiting it to the ground. In March 1994 the U.S. government succeeded in forging a weak Croat-Muslim Federation. While this ended most of the fighting between Croats and the Bosnian government, it escalated the war, because the new Federation promptly launched an offensive against the Bosnian Serbs (Republika Serbska).

Throughout 1994 attempts at moderating the conflict continued as the Contact Group (United States, United Kingdom, France, Germany, Russia) sent its mediators to work with the conflict parties. Although they developed a series of "Zagreb" plans, the three adversaries continued to expand, rotate, and resupply their forces. Former U.S. president Jimmy Carter obtained a Christmas 1994 cease-fire.

### Deescalation and the Peace Agreement

The first successful and lasting deescalatory steps were taken in August 1995, when the president of the Federal Republic and the leaders of the Bosnian Serbs agreed to put aside differences to form a Greater Serbian negotiating team and offered to stop shelling civilian areas in exchange for a halt to NATO bombing. By September 14 all shelling and bombing had ended. At that time, the conflict was being further deescalated by the initiation of serious diplomatic intervention by the Clinton administration and by the stalling of the Croat-Muslim Federation offensive against the Bosnian Serbs. On October 10 a general cease-fire was declared throughout Bosnia. For the first time in four years, the guns fell silent.

Negotiations began in Dayton, Ohio, on November 1 and led to an agreement on November 21 – a moment before their impending collapse.[4] The three main conflict principals formally signed the peace agreement in Paris on December 14. The United States, the European Union, and Russia signed as guarantors of the peace.

The Dayton Agreement was an imposed settlement, with the Bosnian Croats and Bosnian Serbs having much less influence than in earlier negotiations. At Dayton, the presidents of Croatia and the Federal Republic were negotiating for their Bosnian compatriots, who were placed in a take-it-or-leave-it position. The negotiations were marked by a complete lack of trust, suspicion greatly deepened by that long period of escalation. Negotiating leaders expressed surprise that the fighting had continued so long and at such cost. The Bosnian president noted the "mountain of corpses" separating the sides, which made trust impossible. Looking back over those years, the Croatian defense minister resisted giving "away the territory we conquered with Croatian blood" (Holbrooke 1998, 297, 301).

In January 1996 sixty thousand NATO troops began to move into Bosnia, to provide the physical security necessary for implementation of the Dayton Agreement. On February 17 the First Compliance Summit was held in Rome. By March 18 Sarajevo had been administratively reunited as Bosnia's capital.

Conflict continued to subside throughout 1996 as the militant Bosnian Serb leaders progressively ceded their positions to more moderate ones. On September 14, Bosnia's first national elections in five years were held and by December, the joint Bosnian presidency and its institutions were in place, functioning at least minimally. At this writing, Bosnia remains divided into three zones, each controlled by the ethnic majorities residing there. Hundreds of thousands of refugees remain displaced. Order is maintained by NATO and Russian troops – an uneasy "peace" at best.

Although the Dayton agreement was a remarkable accomplishment, this imposed settlement involved the conflict parties much less and with much greater cost than the much earlier Vance-Owen plan would have done. While Dayton did end open coerciveness, it legitimized the three ethnic nationalist parties, making them responsible for implementing the agreement, thereby decreasing the likelihood of a viable multiethnic Bosnia (Kaldor 1999, 67). Still, some observers feel that with a strong international effort, a unified Bosnia is yet possible (Western and Serwer 2000).

## Theoretical Analysis

An analysis of all aspects of this complex conflict with its four conflict groups is possible, but it would not best serve to *illustrate* how our theory can be used to explain escalation and deescalation. A much better approach is to take one important aspect of this conflict and use the theory to explain it. Here we attempt to explain why the Greater Serbs, led by the Serb-dominated Yugoslav People's Army, occupied

Bosnian territory in spring 1992; why they then stopped escalating their coerciveness; and why, later on, they deescalated and, ultimately, accepted a peace accord.

The Serbs are chosen for analysis because they played a crucial role in the conflict, not because we wish to single them out for aggression or atrocities. Our objective is to look at the conflict from their point of view and, in so doing, illustrate how the theory of Chapter 7 can explain their escalating and deescalating actions. We set the stage by considering why the goals of the Serbs were incompatible with those of the Bosnian government.

### Incompatibility of Goals

Because our focus is on the topics of escalation and deescalation, we forgo a detailed analysis of Serb goals and those of their opponents and go immediately to our conclusions. Figure 8.3 shows that the main reason why the goals of the Serbs were incompatible with those of the Bosnian government was a contest over territory: Bosnian Serbs wished the territory occupied by them to be annexed to the Serb-dominated Federal Republic of Yugoslavia, whereas the Bosnian government wished to preserve it as a part of its independent republic.

Figure 8.3 further shows that the main reason for this contest was the gradual disintegration of Yugoslavia: Greater Serbs, who wished to preserve the Federal Republic as a protection for Serbs, viewed an independent republic of Bosnia-Herzegovina as illegitimate; the Bosnian Muslims and Croats, who wished to be freed from Serb domination, asserted their right to govern themselves. Moreover, the Greater Serb's desire to annex parts of Bosnia was fueled by their belligerent culture and ideology: they believed that they had a historic right to these territories.

The two adversaries had incompatible goals for another reason, incompatible values. This incompatibility began when, in the fifteenth century, parts of Bosnia were occupied by the Ottoman Turks, and many Bosnians were converted to Islam; it was further advanced when Tito's policy of decentralization gave Bosnians – Serbs, Croats, and Muslims – a measure of independence.

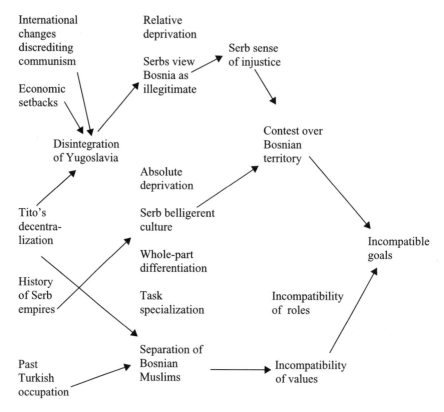

**Figure 8.3.** Main Reasons for Goal Incompatibility in the Greater Serb–Bosnian Conflict

### Emergence of an Open Conflict: Serbian Attack

As we expected (see Figure 5.3), two causes were operating in the Greater Serbs' attack: their high conflict solidarity and their material resources. As their leaders reminded them of their historic grievances against the Muslims and Croats, and as they became increasingly frustrated by the political chaos and economic stress around them, Bosnian Serbs became even more hostile toward the Bosnian Muslims and Croats. This hostility, combined with their belligerent ideology, led to high conflict solidarity. As the theory of Chapter 5 suggests, conflict organization was a more or less natural by-product. But they also had sufficient resources to wage war: they were able to mobilize a force of

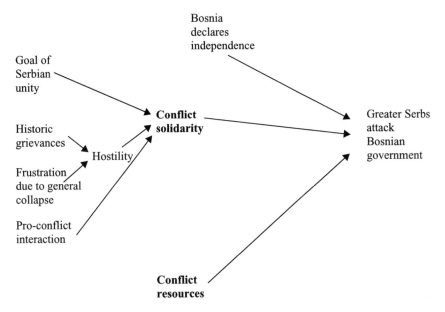

**Figure 8.4.** Reasons for the Greater Serb Attack

eighty thousand, with troops and material support from the Yugoslav People's Army and paramilitaries from the Federal Republic.

Figure 8.4 represents these considerations graphically. Note that, although the diagram applies the theory of Figure 5.3, it omits several of the theory's variables – those not essential to our understanding of the Greater Serb attack. It does show, however, the event that seems to have ignited the explosive situation: the declaration of Bosnian independence.

### *Serb Escalating and Deescalating Actions*

Having considered why the goals of the adversaries were incompatible and why the Greater Serb forces attacked Bosnian government forces, we have prepared the ground for the main topic of this chapter, the escalation and deescalation of the conflict, using the theory shown in Figure 7.1.

Figure 8.2 considered coerciveness resulting from conflict actions by *all* adversaries, including actions such as the Croatian invasion of the Krajina region. But when we limit ourselves to Serb coerciveness – the topic we wish to consider here – we obtain a somewhat different picture. Their coerciveness seems to fall into three distinct periods – escalation, leveling off, and deescalation – which raise three questions. Why did the Greater Serbs escalate their coerciveness in March and April 1992? Why, starting in mid-1992, did they stop their unilateral escalation? Why, in 1994, did they start to deescalate (with an exceptional spike of coercive activity in 1995), ultimately agreeing to end the war?

*Period of Escalation.* According to media reports (e.g., *New York Times,* April 23, 1992), the Greater Serbs – the Yugoslav People's Army, Bosnian Serb irregulars, and paramilitaries from the Federal Republic of Yugoslavia (FRY) known as the Serbian Volunteer Guard – escalated their coerciveness within a month of the referendum supporting Bosnian independence. As Bosnian Serbs established their own Republika Srbska, Greater Serb forces attacked in the south, west and northwest capturing various Bosnian towns and attacking Bosnian Croat areas. After five weeks, they had gained control of more than 60 percent of Bosnia (Ramet 1996, 246) and began to use "ethnic cleansing" – rape, murder, and mass expulsion – to consolidate their hold on the territories they occupied in Bosnia.

  Why did Greater Serbs continue escalating their coerciveness? Evidence suggests that their escalation was due largely to the same conditions that caused them to attack. Their conflict resources in Bosnia remained more than adequate to the task: they had a force of about 80,000 Bosnian Serbs with support from a Yugoslav People's Army of 89,000, while the Bosnian government had a force of only about 50,000. And Greater Serb conflict solidarity remained high, as is shown by the fact that Greater Serb leader Milosevic remained popular and had been easily reelected in December 1991.

  To understand Serb escalation even better, let us consider how these original conditions (abundant resources and high conflict solidarity) affected the three components of escalation (reciprocation, hostility, and unilateral escalation). Because the Greater Serbs' opponents were very weak, *reciprocation* ($rO$) played only a minor part. (This is because when Opponent's coerciveness $O$ is low, the tendency to reciprocate, $rO$, is low as well.) On the other hand, *hostility* toward Bosnian

Muslims continued to contribute to the Serbs' escalation: the secession of Bosnia made them more apprehensive, and the government of the Federal Republic continued telling them that they were victims with enemies on all sides (Crnobrnja 1994).

But it appears that the Serbs' tendency to escalate *unilaterally* fostered their coerciveness more than anything else. Driven by a desire to create Greater Serbia, they endeavored to establish a continuous arc of Serb-held territory in Bosnia contiguous with the Federal Republic (Rogel 1998, 32). Moreover, their militant ideology – an important component of conflict solidarity – suggested that they should use all available force to reach their goal. It glorified their past, called for unification of all Serbs, and justified attacks in Bosnia as merely restoring territory that was rightly theirs. It also justified their atrocities against Bosnian Croats and Muslims. In fact, there is some evidence that even the raping of Bosnian women was calculated to make the conquered territories purely Serbian (Ramet 1996, 258).

Thus, to a large extent, Serb escalation during the first five weeks of open warfare was driven primarily by the original conditions: abundant resources and high conflict solidarity. But new factors were promoting escalation even further – feedbacks from the conflict.

One of the feedbacks created conditions that made *strategic* escalation desirable: Bosnian government forces were getting stronger by the minute,[5] and the United Nations was preparing to apply more stringent sanctions against the Greater Serbs. These threats made it imperative that they should hurry, conquering and pacifying the territory they sought. The second feedback was from *atrocities*. Some of them had been committed against Serbs in the Croatian civil war, but many in that war were committed by Serbs themselves. For example, in early 1991 Serbs killed and mutilated Croatian police after promising them safe passage into a violence-ridden village (Ramet 1996, 50). As Figure 7.2 suggests, when a party commits atrocities, social psychological processes are activated to justify them, and further violence becomes routine.

*Period of Relative Stability.* From mid-1992 to the beginning of 1994, Bosnian Serbs, while maintaining a high level of conflict activity, largely abstained from escalating the military conflict unilaterally.[6] When they did escalate, it was mostly in response to attacks by their opponents. Why this change?

Chapter 7 suggests that a conflict party can stop escalating for two main reasons: either because it has reached an equilibrium or because it is influenced by feedbacks from the conflict. Because the Serbs were very belligerent, they were already engaged in a runaway escalation without an equilibrium. (Recall that when a party is very belligerent, its parameter $u$ is, by definition, negative. And, as shown in Figure 7.2, that leads to runaway escalation.) Therefore, their tendency to escalate *unilaterally* must have been diminished, most likely because of some feedbacks they received. Because there is little evidence that Serb solidarity – the first of the two possible feedbacks (see Figure 7.3) – had decreased, it appears that they stopped escalating because of events that made a new approach *strategically* advisable (the second possible feedback).

After the first five weeks, a long series of events began to occur. On one hand, the Serbs had already reached most of their territorial objectives; on the other, the forces of the Bosnian government were becoming larger than those of the Bosnian Serbs who, by then, had lost the military support of their Greater Serb allies. Moreover, the international community had begun to intervene in the conflict: the Federal Republic of Yugoslavia was expelled from the UN, and economic sanctions against it were imposed. NATO established a "no fly zone" for Yugoslav aircraft, the UN sent in peace-keeping troops, an international war crimes tribunal was established, and various peace plans were formulated.

The relatively short episodes of Serb escalation during this period were mostly a matter of *retaliation*. Unfortunately, some actions that provoked it were due to well-meaning but ill-conceived international efforts. When the UN dispatched a humanitarian intervention force to Bosnia in August 1992, Serbs retaliated by holding UN personnel hostage and obstructing the flow of relief supplies. When, in March 1994, the U.S. government succeeded in forging a weak Croat-Muslim Federation, the federation launched an offensive against Bosnian Serbs, thus provoking Serb retaliation.

*Period of Deescalation.* The turning point for Serb coerciveness appears to have occurred when, in February 1994, Bosnian Serbs shelled a

Sarajevo marketplace, creating a bloody massacre that was widely tele-
vised throughout the world (Rogel 1998, 35), greatly increasing international hostility against the Serbs. The UN and NATO increased
their coercive efforts, giving the Serbs an ultimatum to evacuate a
twenty-kilometer exclusion zone around Sarajevo and shooting down
four Serbian planes. At first, Serb forces retaliated by violating the
NATO-proclaimed safe areas, expelling Western journalists, abducting
UN troops, fire-bombing UN relief offices in Belgrade, and shooting
down a British plane (Rogel 1998, 36). But, ultimately, they began serious deescalation. Once again, *strategic* considerations played a decisive
role.

Deescalation became advisable when the so-called Contact Group
succeeded in driving a wedge between Bosnian Serbs and the Federal
Republic. The group accomplished this by promising the latter that
the sanctions against it would be eased if it distanced itself from the
Bosnian Serbs. When Belgrade began to do so, by accusing the Bosnian
Serbs of being "killers of civilians" and by prohibiting trade with them,
this promise was kept. The group also rewarded Bosnian Croats –
who by 1993 had begun fighting the Bosnian government forces – for
agreeing to tolerate continued UN presence on their territory, with
an implied promise that the Bosnian territory they occupied would be
theirs to keep.[7]

In November 1995 the all-important peace talks in Dayton began.
During these negotiations, the three conflict groups – the Greater
Serbs, the Greater Croats, and the Muslim Bosnian government –
were housed separately, with U.S. officials shuttling between them
and twisting arms whenever necessary. Difficult as the talks were, the
Dayton Agreement was reached and initialed on November 21, 1995.
It created a two-part state: a Muslim-Croat federation would control
51 percent of the territory, the Bosnian Serbs' Republika Serbska the
remaining 49 percent. There would be a central government and presidency as well as legislative and executive bodies within each part (Rogel
1998, 40).

Why did the Greater Serbs agree to this settlement? Once again,
strategic considerations prevailed: with one major exception – the city
of Sarajevo – they ended controlling the territory they wanted; they
received international recognition of a Bosnian Serb republic; and
they were under intense international pressure to end the conflict.

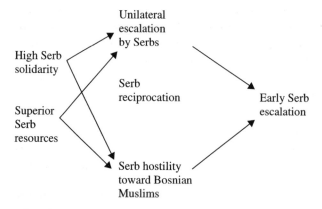

**Figure 8.5.** Reasons for Early Serb Escalation

*Conclusions.* Escalation by the Greater Serbs during the first part of the war was due mostly to the momentum created by the conditions that made them use military force in Bosnia in the first place. Thus Figure 8.5, a simplified and augmented version of Figure 8.4,[8] shows that, at the beginning of the conflict, the Bosnian Serbs *escalated* their military actions primarily because they had high solidarity and superior resources. Their conflict solidarity was high because it was based on a belligerent ideology; their military forces were superior both in numbers and training.

Specifically, Figure 8.5 suggests that high solidarity and military superiority led Greater Serbs to escalate unilaterally and that their escalation was also due to their hostility toward both Muslims and Croats. This hostility, combined with their militant culture and ideology, explains why they resorted to ethnic cleansing of the conquered territories. Reciprocation, on the other hand, did not play an important role because Bosnian government forces offered only minor resistance during this period. But the force and fury of Serb conflict actions can be understood fully only if we consider certain *feedbacks* from the conflict. Figure 8.6, an applied version of Figure 7.5, suggests that, while the conflict had little effect on the Serbs' solidarity, it did create threats that had to be dealt with: they were in danger of losing their military superiority, and were threatened with UN-NATO intervention. It was

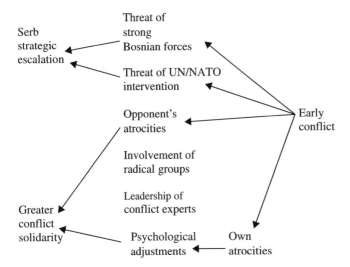

**Figure 8.6.** Feedbacks Amplifying Serb Escalation

therefore strategically advisable for the Serbs to strike quickly, while they had military superiority.

Why did the Serbs later deescalate their conflict behavior, ultimately agreeing to a negotiated settlement? Chapter 7 argued that when deescalation follows escalation, at least one of three possible feedbacks must have occurred: the conflict has created conditions that make deescalation strategically advisable, it has decreased the group's conflict solidarity, or it has decreased its resources.

Figure 8.7, an applied version of Figure 7.6, summarizes our interpretations of Serb *deescalation*. It shows that strategic considerations – rather than decreased solidarity – were primarily responsible: by that time, Bosnian Serbs were already outnumbered by the Bosnian government forces; they began to lose support of their Federal Republic allies; they faced an increasingly powerful UN-NATO intervention; and they had to consider a variety of peace proposals.

## The Bosnian Conflict Reconsidered

We observed some classic stimuli of escalation at work in the Bosnian conflict. We saw how escalation builds from one event to the next, from

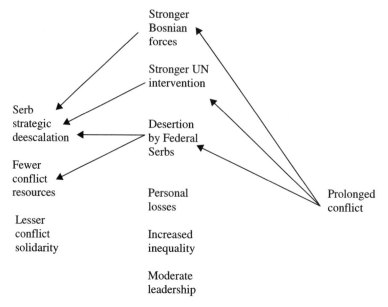

**Figure 8.7.** Feedbacks Leading to Serb Deescalation

one level of coerciveness to a higher one. In the Croatian war, Greater Croats and Greater Serbs had committed numerous physical and cultural atrocities upon one another. Ethnic cleansing, bombardment of civilians, and destruction of cultural monuments all occurred there, well before they did in Bosnia. Because such hostility was created in Croatia, the Greater Croats and Greater Serbs were more ready to take revenge and ensure conflict solidarity against opponents in Bosnia. By 1993 Bosnian Muslims were also ready to retaliate for the Serb and Croat violence against them.

We saw, too, how the range of choices becomes narrowed by earlier escalatory decisions and events. For example, at first the Bosnian government had been willing to preserve Yugoslavia and to remain within it. But the secessions of Slovenia, Macedonia, and Croatia, and the retaliatory response of Belgrade to them, raised Bosnian hostility, economic insecurity, and fear to a level that made a declaration of independence inevitable. Especially influential in that declaration was the Greater Serbs' political and military activity within Bosnia.

We also saw how during this period certain catalytic events and conditions affected the formation of conflict groups and ethnic solidarity, and the dynamics of escalation. As Bosnia, a country completely surrounded by Croatia and the Federal Republic, underwent increasing economic stress from its geographic isolation, its ethnic divisions deepened. Bosnian Croats saw their future security increasingly with Greater Croatia rather than with an independent Bosnia. Bosnian Serbs likewise felt more and more a part of Greater Serbia. Economic and social ties with the outside eclipsed those with the Bosnian homeland. The most influential development, however, was the militarization of the conflict: the sending of weapons to and the training of their Bosnian compatriots by both Croatia and the Federal Republic.

These developments illustrate several important points about escalation. First, they show how the process builds on itself, how momentum and the dynamics of retaliation quickly take the conflict out of the hands of those who might otherwise control it. Second, they suggest the centrality and often the unintended consequences of impartial third-party activities, such as interposition, mediation, and humanitarian relief. Although third-party intervention is normally intended to moderate a conflict, under certain conditions the presence of an impartial third party can actually stimulate it, as did UN troops taken hostage late in the conflict. Third, we learn from the Bosnian case the importance of intervening early to control escalation. The longer escalation proceeds, the more momentum builds, the greater harm opponents do to one another, and the greater are the costs each sinks into the conflict, to be regained by each in the future at the other's expense.

The conflict in Bosnia, so poorly managed by all involved, was expensive not only in its direct human consequences but also in its consequences for later escalation in nearby Kosovo. At each stage of the Bosnian escalation, minorities felt shut out of decisions determining their identity and security, and this exclusion reinforced their sense of being threatened, victimized, unfairly treated, besieged. Each new escalation visited new suffering and generated new unwillingness to settle on all sides. The treatment of the Serb minority in Croatia had convinced Bosnian Serbs they could not trust their future to others in a multiethnic Bosnia. As the Bosnian Muslims had become a territorial minority through Serb and Croatian cleansing, they were reluctant to settle at Dayton and had to be coerced into doing so.

Conflict escalation in Bosnia later engendered that same escalation in the Kosovo region of the Federal Republic. The mistreatment of Muslims in the Bosnian conflict, particularly by Serbs, inflamed Albanian Muslim nationalism and militarism. Especially when their problematic future was ignored in the Dayton Agreement, Albanian Kosovars shifted away from well-organized civil protest (Clark 2000) toward armed resistance to the Serbian government, and civil war was under way there by 1997. The Serb minority in Kosovo was also increasingly fearful, perceiving itself as part of a threatened Serbian nation being engulfed by an Islamic Albania.

Finally, the failure of the European Union states and the United States to intervene with resolve earlier in the Bosnian escalation produced a strong sense of guilt among the leaders and peoples of those nations. A serious military intervention by NATO in 1995 seemed to have brought a deescalation of the Bosnian conflict. Why shouldn't it work again, in Kosovo? Those organizations were thus encouraged to use such one-sided military intervention early in the Kosovo conflict, under very different conditions. Massive NATO bombing of the Federal Republic led not to peaceful resolution but to a mass exodus of refugees and great material destruction and some loss of life, and produced no peace and little stability in the region.

Of course, the escalation of conflict in Kosovo was not solely an outcome of that in Bosnia. But one is tempted to speculate on how the Bosnian conflict might have been dealt with at much less cost had escalation there been reversed much earlier and what effect an earlier Bosnian settlement might have had in Kosovo.

The international community is now struggling to develop more effective, less costly intervention approaches out of the experience and hindsight of the 1990s (Miall, Ramsbotham, and Woodhouse 1999). It must work with some sobering, largely unsuccessful experiences in Rwanda, Somalia, Bosnia, Kosovo, and East Timor.

In reviewing the path of the conflict in Bosnia, one is struck by the swiftness with which everyday life was carried away by momentum and panic: once escalation had begun, multiethnic communities that had lived together in relative peace for centuries were torn apart by a mere suggestion of military attack. One must ask whether there are ways to build a sense of security in such communities that might immunize them against such inhuman and unjust policies as were visited upon Bosnian civilians.

# CHAPTER NINE

# Making Conflict Work
# Economically

SO FAR, we have explored theories that help us understand why a conflict comes into being and grows. We saw that often this understanding helps us to deal with a conflict in its latent stage. But many problems cannot be solved entirely by addressing their root causes. For example, to fight a large fire, we seldom need to know how it got started; what we need is fire-fighting equipment and fire fighters who know how to use it. Similarly, while knowing how a conflict started is often essential, we also need conflict-moderating skills that are as specialized as those of a fire fighter.

In this chapter, we discuss theories useful for conflict actors: those who are actively involved in the conflict. While some of our discussion could be seen as a restatement of the theories we have already considered, some of it formulates new principles. We focus on approaches that can help one determine how to minimize costs of a conflict.

There are three main approaches to moderating conflict: preventing serious, unnecessary conflict at its points of origin; moving inevitable conflict toward cooperation as it emerges; and moderating coercive conflict as it escalates.

## Preventing Serious Conflict

Because incompatibility of goals is a major source of conflict, a society can lessen conflict by addressing the main causes of incompatible goals: social injustice, role conflict, and value differences (see Chapter 3). But a society can also build into itself a tolerance for "healthy" conflict. Simmel (Coser 1956) argued that both attraction and repulsion between groups are essential for social integration and continuity. A healthy society, organization, or group maintains a balance of cooperative and oppositional relations.

If a society looks upon conflict as both friend and foe, it has a better chance of preventing serious and costly types of conflict. Analytic conflict theory has much to teach us about the dual nature of conflict. Simmel observed that social conflict may be as important for a healthy society as cooperation. All group relations have positive elements of attraction and negative ones of repulsion. Association and dissociation are facts of social life. The forces of social integration, however, usually tend to outweigh those that force us apart. Society wants to stay together and thus ignores or suppresses conflict rather than acknowledging and using it. Simmel would argue that social education should pay as much attention to conflict's positive functions as to its dysfunctions. Human society should be as inventive about ways of engaging in conflict at minimal cost to all – nation-states, groups, individuals – as it is about getting its members to cooperate. The more inventive it is, the less likely that inevitable social tensions will produce high-cost conflict.

Because low-intensity conflicts are rarely encouraged, we discuss four ways to increase their use: balanced sociation, consultation, effective communication, and reconciling potential conflict groups through free interaction.

### Balanced Sociation

Balanced sociation is a conscious effort by a society to make both cooperation and conflict prominent in public consciousness, formal education, and public investment. The assumption is that a continuing tension between the two is important for stable and productive social relations. Aho (1994) speaks of "tension wisdom" developing within a society like the United States, with its members growing increasingly tolerant of disagreements and differences and learning how to live with them more creatively and productively.

Balanced sociation could be strengthened through a society's education process. Skills at opposing constructively could be taught alongside those of cooperating and getting along. Relations with one's opponent would be understood in both their associative and their dissociative dimensions. Both coercive and cooperative conflict resolution would be taught as art forms in the schools. Mediators, arbitrators, national defense specialists, and other conflict professionals would learn how to balance sociation and use conflict in their work.

One guarantor of balanced sociation is what Coser (1956) called the "safety valve" mechanisms – institutions permitting social and interpersonal conflict at minimal cost: nonviolent social movements; institutional third parties such as court systems and mediators; ritualized conflict in sport; and training in noninjurious defense and fighting methods such as the martial arts.

One increasingly common form of social action that illustrates both balanced sociation and safety valve conflict is civil disobedience: an individual or group refuses to obey certain laws but also refuses to use violence against those who enforce them. Since the 1960s, U.S. society has become increasingly tolerant of nonviolent conflict action, recognizing it as a useful safety valve that leads to necessary social change at minimal cost.

The southern sit-ins of the 1960s demonstrated how civil disobedience and other forms of nonviolent action can bring about a society that is more just and less vulnerable to upheaval (Wehr 1968). Black student protest, guided by the Southern Christian Leadership Conference, dealt with highly emotional conflict at low cost to society. Likewise, in the 1970s and 1980s, large numbers of North Americans and Europeans used nonviolent action to oppose their governments' preparations for nuclear war. For nearly two decades, the citizens movement against the Rocky Flats nuclear weapons plant in Colorado used disciplined nonviolent protest to influence public opinion, government officials, legislators, and plant workers (Downton and Wehr 1997). As with the civil rights sit-ins, a conflict with great emotional content and potential for high cost was moderated by such nonviolent direct action, and the governments and publics of many nations were moved toward necessary change. A comparison of how mass public protest was handled in Chicago in 1968 and Seattle in 1999 suggests that U.S. society has learned something of the value of safety valve conflict but still has much to learn.

## Consultation

Even in societies that acknowledge and teach balanced sociation as an explicit principle of healthy social relations, many groups' interests will be potentially in conflict. They will continue to see many of their goals as incompatible with those of others. Some goals will truly be so while other interests will only appear to be. Helping groups to distinguish actual from illusory goal incompatibility is a promising strategy for conflict prevention.

True goals and interests are often obscured when decisions are made for a group rather than with it. Usually the more powerful ignore or forget the need for consultation with those they control, thus producing unnecessary misunderstanding and resentment. Hierarchical structures, such as one finds in rigid class societies or in bureaucratic organizations, also tend to hinder consultation. This results partly from power differences between levels and partly from communication patterns tending to run horizontally rather than vertically. The segregated South of the 1950s, where the needs and feelings of large segments of the population were disregarded by those in power, is a particularly good illustration.

Increasing consultation among potential conflict groups need not involve major redistribution of power, though it could lead there over time (Curle 1971). It might simply involve creating a more consultative decision process. Just sounding out all those to be directly affected by a decision usually reduces the likelihood of conflict potential. Consultation helps reveal where true goal incompatibility exists and where it does not.

## Effective Communication

Preventing conflict through consultation requires effective communication. As communicators send and receive messages, there is enormous opportunity for slippage in the sequence of what is meant, said, heard, or understood (Hocker and Wilmot 1991). We are sometimes amazed at how what we meant to say was so misunderstood. Words and their accompanying nonverbal messages often contradict one another (Tillett 1991).

*Misunderstanding.* Social conflict nearly always involves misunderstanding. Conflict parties communicate both by what they say or fail to say, and by how they behave toward one another. Even normal interaction involves some faulty communication, but conflict seems to increase it. The higher the level of conflict, the more costly misunderstanding may be. During the Cold War, miscommunication between U.S. and Soviet leaders could have had catastrophic consequences. At every stage and level of conflict, clear communication among parties usually reduces unwise decisions by and costs for the participants.

As a conflict emerges, adversaries become more emotional. Anger, fear, hostility, and suspicion all make communicators more likely to send and receive faulty messages to and from their opponents and their supporters alike. Emotion control is one way to encourage accuracy. The context of the communication is also important. The more background noise and distraction, the less clear the message. The pace and difficulty of message exchange also influence how long and carefully one considers a message before responding to it. For example, a conflict among a university's physics faculty intensified as participants dashed off e-mail responses to one another, unrestrained by slower, more direct, and more demanding nonelectronic ways of communicating. Conversely, when the parties can verify their communication, they tend to increase its accuracy.

*Sending and Listening Skills.* For written communications, conflict parties should use a message checker – someone who will ask what they wish to convey and whether it will actually be heard that way by the recipient. This checking is often done incidentally, but building it formally into the communication process would give it the prominence it deserves. Much misunderstanding is created simply by careless and imprecise use of words.

The more hostile communication is, the less accurately it may be heard. Hostility produces a defensive reaction by the receiver, who is then less likely to pick up nuances that give a message greater clarity. An important skill is knowing how to use "disarming" rather than "arming" language. The latter selects more forceful words, uses statements rather than questions, and is usually accompanied by hostile intonations, accusatory pauses, and other nonverbal messages that convey hostile feeling.

Methods have been developed to overcome obstacles to effective communication. With "I messages," for example, the sender clarifies the intended meaning of the message.[1] Such messages locate the conflict outside the listener, where it can more easily be reframed for cooperative resolution. They often expand the opponent's ability to listen and hear. They also focus on behavior rather than the person as the source of the conflict. Less likely to be felt as personal attacks, they encourage a similar "I" response from the other.

Often a conflict party is less interested in being clearly understood than in having its say. If its opponent is similarly motivated, a war of words with little clear communication is probable. However, having one's say is a necessary first step toward mutual disclosure and emotional openness. For this reason, disarming listening may be as useful as using disarming language. The technique of "active listening" (Hocker and Wilmot 1991, 239) has several functions. First, it permits the venting of emotion: the speaker feels heard, and tension is released. The listener's body posture and gestures, such as head nodding, confirm for the speaker the sense of being heard. Next, the speaker's feelings are restated by the listener, who paraphrases what the speaker has said, checking with him for accuracy. He or she then asks clarifying questions for further information. The telling-listening function is extremely important in conflict resolution, particularly where a continuing relationship between the parties is necessary, whether they be divorcing parents or ethnic communities in Bosnia and Kosovo.

*An Example.* Consider the following scenario. Ruth is a senior manager in a government department. Her deputy, John, was one of the applicants for the position she holds, and he was very angry when he was not appointed. John treats Ruth in a formal, unfriendly, but polite manner. He carries out her instructions precisely but never does more than she explicitly tells him. Believing that the tension between them is destructive, both for her and for the workplace, Ruth decides to meet with John in an attempt to clear the air. Although he agrees to the meeting, he insists that there is no problem, that his treatment of her is entirely appropriate, and that he has no wish to have any sort of informal or personal relationship with her (Tillett 1991, 31).

How might Ruth communicate in her upcoming meeting with her deputy to reduce tension between them? First, she would ask herself where it should take place. The physical setting can help or hinder communication. His coming to her office would emphasize the status difference and the related resentment already blocking communication. Her visiting his office might seem contrived. As neutral and businesslike a setting as possible would be recommended here. Second, Ruth would describe the tension she feels between them and ask John what he thinks might be done to reduce it. Such an approach might induce him to disclose more of his own feelings. The "I" messages and active listening methods she can use would tend to personalize their communication sufficiently but not to a degree that would be uncomfortable for him. Finally, she might ask him to design a program for improving communication generally in the department. In so doing, he would become a resident specialist in it, and thus a deputy with special status.

### Reconciling Potential Conflict Groups

Chapter 5 suggests that conflict groups emerge when those with seemingly incompatible goals limit interaction to people within their group, so that each group develops a separate identity and consequent solidarity. By the same token, reconciliation within a society will be enhanced and the formation of conflict groups reduced if conditions are created that encourage free interaction across the boundaries of such potential conflict groups. Such interaction may work to decrease incompatibility: their members may begin to like each other, creating similar interests and goals.

*Interaction Rituals.* Goffman's (1967) concept of "interaction ritual" provides us with an understanding of how free interaction can prevent conflict across racial and class divisions. Interaction rituals occur when members of a group – a civil rights organization, for example – are in close proximity to each other (meetings and demonstrations) and have a common focus of attention (racial justice), and when their interaction is imbued with deep feelings (shared humanity). Such interactions tend to transform the members' common reality into something sacred, signifying membership in a common group, and providing a reference point of moral solidarity for the whole group. Such rituals may either promote or block a group's ties to other groups.

As an example, consider an exchange of musicians or dancers between two hostile nations. When the visiting artists perform, the close proximity of members of the audience, their attention to the performers, and the feelings stirred by the performance create a bond between the audience, the artists, and the nations they represent. As another example, consider the civil rights movement. As whites joined the civil rights movement of the early 1960s, black-white interaction rituals were being created that celebrated interracial unity; subsequently, as the black power and black pride movement developed, new rituals of solidarity and membership among blacks alone eclipsed those that encouraged interracial bonds.

Bonding rituals might be useful in Bosnian communities that still have multiethnic populations. One might encourage small group discussions between Muslims and Roman Catholics dealing with topics of local health and safety and the merits of candidates in upcoming elections. Such interactions might become "ritualized," celebrating the sacredness of the larger urban community, bonds of citizenship as Bosnians, and the like. They could offset the rituals occurring within each religious community and thus discourage divisive ethnic communalism.

*Social Reality Construction.* As conflict emerges, opponents are very likely to misperceive the other's goals, motives, and attributes. As the role of enemy is thrust upon one's opponent, he or she is seen as behaving pretty much as one would expect an opponent to do. A self-fulfilling prophecy begins to operate and the perceived enemy becomes a real one. Opposing sides create the conflict in part by how they make sense of what is happening between them. Conflict reality depends heavily on how the conflict parties explain to themselves and others what is going on. The parties may see their respective goals as highly incompatible where in fact they are not. Acting from such misperceptions may in fact make them so.

How humans explain what is happening as they interact is important for understanding social conflict. Berger and Luckmann (1966) see any interaction as created socially by the conflict parties out of their everyday activity. In conflicts this process of social creation happens as we first externalize what we believe is happening. Thus, when we make a new friend (or enemy), we create a relationship. We recreate it each time we interact with that friend (or enemy). For example, two physicists often have need for the same lab space, equipment, and graduate student at the same time. On one such occasion, they may have a nasty encounter with personal insults. From that time forward, the joint problem of scarce resources may be redefined by them as a conflict.

The new product (friendship or conflict) is then objectified as it fits into the descriptive terminology and other parts of the objective order society already has in place to describe such interactions. We internalize that new objective reality, feeling that it fits our experience, and we act accordingly. It thus becomes reality for us even though our perception is at odds with the facts. Each conflict becomes a clash of contending realties, with opponents convinced it is factually based.

Getting conflict parties to question their perception of reality permits them to distinguish those aspects of reality that are in opposition from those that are not. Once the parties realize that they are not in total conflict with one another, they can begin to cooperate and turn the conflicting interests into a problem to be solved. If a conflict is a reality constructed by opponents, it can just as well be reconstructed by them into less costly, more cooperative forms.

Enemy images are the most harmful and resistant form of constructed conflict reality. One believes and expects the worst of an enemy. Getting opponents to reconstruct their "enemy" perception of each other has been the focus of several enemy reality reconstruction projects carried on by academic researchers.

Among the first experiments with getting opponents to question their perception of a conflict reality were Burton's (1969) *controlled communication workshops*. He brought representatives of nations and societies who were hostile to each other to a program of intense examination of their perceptions of objective reality and of one another. He used a range of exercises, including optical illusion graphics, to get participants to question their beliefs about what was real.

Herbert Kelman has brought together young academicians and diplomats from opposing sides in a conflict – with Palestinians and Israelis (Kelman 1982), for example. In his approach he attempts to sensitize participants to the problem realities faced by their opponents.

Mitchell and Banks (1996, 145) reviewed scholar-practitioner approaches that have, as their central theme, reconstructing reality and that strive to transform the participants into enhanced realists who know with greater clarity the nature of the conflict situation they confront. They concluded that reality reconstruction workshops have a special problem: reentering from the workshop setting into the conflict situation participants temporarily left behind. There will be an inevitable disconnection between the reality reconstructed in the workshop and the unreconstructed reality to which the parties return. Even their workshop participation may be seen as fraternizing with the enemy and may place them at personal risk, as was apparently the case with some in the Doob (Doob and Foltz 1974) intervention in the conflict in Northern Ireland. Those who are external to the conflict must enter it with great caution, because there always are constituencies to whom participants must answer, and whose realities may remain unreconstructed.

Some progress in reconstructing enemy realities has been reported in programs where leaders are brought together without being extracted from their constituent communities. The Public Conversations program in Boston, for example, has had some success in reducing at least local hostility around the abortion issue (Chasin et al. 1996). There, enemies have become partners working on reducing abortion through preventing unwanted pregnancies, an approach acceptable to both. All enemies have some common reality, certain goals all of them wish to achieve. Identifying that common ground through reality reconstruction is an important step.

## Moving toward Cooperation

Conflict can take either a cooperative or coercive path (Deutsch and Coleman 2000). Which direction it takes depends on how it is "framed" by the conflict parties. If they characterize it as a problem solvable through their joint effort, cooperative approaches – such as negotiation – will be adopted early on. If, however, the conflict is seen as a win-lose struggle, coercive processes – such as power contests – will likely be the initial strategy of choice.

### Reframing the Conflict

The so-called framing process can limit the cost of conflict. Mediators normally begin it by getting opposing parties to redefine a conflict each has already framed as a "zero-sum" (what one gains the other loses) struggle. Reframing participants' perception of the conflict can lead them to consider a number of cooperative conflict resolution techniques. In order to understand these techniques, let us consider the basic process through which cooperation can be achieved, the process of negotiation.

*Negotiation.* Negotiation occurs when conflict parties agree to meet face-to-face to resolve their conflict. Although various approaches to negotiation have been discussed, so-called integrative bargaining (Fisher and Ury 1981) has been widely accepted as one of the most promising.

Integrative bargaining starts from the assumption that the interests of the conflict parties are seldom totally opposed to one another, that quite often there are common interests not being considered. It approaches negotiation as joint problem solving, a process that permits all negotiators to discover common interests, to identify ways to "increase the size of the pie" available, and even to "bake" more pies. Its goal is to identify the true interests of negotiators, and to build an agreement that meets those interests. It differs from the more conventional and costly "positional bargaining," where positions, demands, and subsequent mutual concessions are inherent in the process.

Integrative bargaining occurs in several stages. It begins with settling the "people problem" by establishing good personal relations and communication among the negotiators. It then moves to getting the negotiators to clarify their interests and leave their stated positions behind.[2] The third stage tries to meet their common and divergent interests collaboratively through joint brainstorming and creation of new options. Although most interests usually are addressed at this third stage, unresolved issues can be considered in the final stage, by applying what Fisher and Ury call "fair standards" – such as precedent or expert judgment – to proposed agreements.

There was a point early in the Bosnian conflict where approaches such as integrative bargaining might have prevented the heavy costs of civil war. The window of opportunity was not large, probably somewhere in mid-1991, before the Yugoslav People's Army decided that its future lay with a Serbian Yugoslavia and thus began to arm Serbian groups in Bosnia. The Croatian government did likewise with Bosnian

Croats. There was a period of a very few months, however, when the more moderate leaders of the Serb, Croat, and Muslim communities in Bosnia might have negotiated an approach to immunize that multiethnic state against such interethnic violence as subsequently occurred.

Several concepts and theories help us to understand why integrative bargaining tends to work well. Prominent among them are the concepts of trust and fairness.

*Promoting Trust.* Integrative bargaining provides negotiators with a process that, through personal sharing, can build trust by eliminating various emotional and communication obstacles. Trust can be further strengthened when a negotiator's verbal and nonverbal communications coincide. In every social encounter, each of us presents a positive "face," or image of self, composed of attributes of which we feel society approves. In other words, we all try to look our best. In the negotiation setting, for example, our best face would likely be conciliatory, powerful, firm, confident, fair, efficient, deserving, and so on. Our success as a negotiator will depend largely on how well we maintain our "negotiating face," how credible it is to our opponent across the table. We maintain it through what Goffman calls "face work" – the actions "taken by a person to make whatever he [or she] is doing consistent with face" (1967, 12). In negotiation, above all, we want our opponents to take us seriously. The more they can be reassured that our face truly represents a reliable negotiating self behind it, the more likely they are to respond likewise and with confidence, and move toward agreement.

People can learn how to act as credible negotiators – in fact, how to *be* credible negotiators.[3] They can be trained in the "face skill" components of negotiation: facial expressions and other body language, voice intonation, conciliatory physical gestures, timing, face saving, and so on. The trust of one's negotiating partner is achieved in large part by a credible performance.

*Fairness in Negotiation.* Two criteria can be applied to settlements: we can attempt to make them "just," or we can strive to make them "best possible." A settlement may be said to be just if it conforms to some universally accepted and invariant principle. Zartman et al. (1996) distinguish among three main principles of fairness: priority, equality, and proportionality.

The *priority* principle usually identifies a winner, and does so by applying an external principle or precedent. For example, the adversaries in the Israeli-Palestinian conflict were using, for many years, the priority principle when the Israelis demanded complete security (an external principle) and the Palestinians demanded the return of all conquered territories (the precedent of previous occupation). The *equality* principle postulates that the adversaries should receive equal shares. This principle was applied to the Israeli-Palestinian conflict when, in 1967, the United Nations Security Council recommended an exchange of territory for security (Zartman et al. 1996, 91).

The *proportionality* principle – also known as the "equity" principle – prescribes that the adversaries be rewarded in proportion to their merit or need. Homans's (1974) concept of distributive justice, discussed in Chapter 3, assumes that rewards should be proportional to an actor's merit: the greater her contributions and investments, the greater her share should be. To illustrate, consider divorce settlements. It is customary to award the primary custody of the children to the mother because, more often than not, she has provided the children with more of the day-to-day care than the husband has (greater contributions), and because, being a woman and a mother, she is more deserving (greater investment).

The settlement may be said to be the *best possible* if it is acceptable to both adversaries and gives them equal measures of (dis)satisfaction. (This suggests that a search for the best possible settlement relies heavily on the equality principle.) But, before this principle can be applied, the adversaries themselves have to be made equal in some fashion.

Several equalizing *procedures* can be applied in real-life conflicts. One of them is that each adversary should reveal his "bottom-line demand" (the option that has zero payoff for him). The equality principle is then applied by "splitting the difference" between these two demands.[4] One could argue that the Dayton Agreement, discussed in Chapter 8, was such a settlement. We might say that the Greater Serbs' bottom-line demand was an annexation of all the territory they had occupied; and that the Bosnian government's bottom-line demand was for control of all of its territory. We might also say that the disappointments of the two sides were commensurate: while 49 percent of Bosnia became a Serbian republic, Sarajevo was not a part of it, and the Greater Serbs could not annex that territory; the Bosnian government, while keeping nominal control over the entire territory and real control over 51 percent of Bosnia, could not reach the goal of keeping all of Bosnia under its exclusive control.

Another major equalizing procedure relies on *equal concessions*. This procedure can be justified on the grounds that, no matter how different the adversaries may be in other respects, their differences can disappear once they make certain prominent demands – such as their opening demands or their bottom-line demands. One can say, in effect, "Now the two are the same: both have made their prominent demands." And, having thus "equalized" them, one can apply the equality principle by insisting that they make equal concessions.

To return to our case of the sit-ins for civil rights, fairness for African Americans was rare in the South of the 1960s. None felt that more keenly than black college students. Resentment of the injustice of state-enforced racial discrimination was acknowledged as the primary motivation for their protest (Wehr 1968, 68). Blacks' negotiation over the method and pace of desegregation began only when the federal government began to implement equality before the law – a principle reflecting the norm of reciprocity.

### Institutionalizing Cooperative Conflict

It is evident that conflict can be limited and controlled by institutional forms (e.g., collective bargaining, the judicial system), social roles (e.g., mediators, conciliators, referees, judges, police), social norms (fairness, justice, equality, nonviolence, integrity of communication), rules for conducting negotiations (such as when to initiate and terminate negotiations, how to set an agenda, or how to present demands), and specific procedures (e.g., hinting versus explicit communication, or public versus private sessions) (Deutsch 1973, 377).

The creation of the U.S. Mediation and Conciliation Service in the 1930s is a good illustration of such institutionalization. Over the decades since then, this service has intervened to transform industrial warfare characterized by threat-heavy conflict strategies into a trading process of collective bargaining. Threat is still used in industrial relations – unions threaten to strike, companies threaten to move their plants elsewhere – but it has been replaced by exchange as the dominant guiding principle.

In the 1960s civil rights conflict, the Community Relations Office was set up in the U.S. Department of Justice to move the conflict parties' emphasis on threat strategies toward exchange and integrative action. It was often quite successful and continues to this day to facilitate racial peace. Civil rights groups in the 1960s already had a threat-minimizing strategy in place with their commitment to nonviolence, although it tended to weaken over the decade as civil rights organizations had to compete with black power groups for the allegiance of black youth.

Conflict-moderating institutions have had a similar influence at the international level. In the 1980s and 1990s, a Central American presidents' organization brought about such a shift away from threats in several civil wars through its Esquipulas peace process. Such change in the strategic power mixes of conflict groups was particularly noticeable in the Nicaraguan conflict (Wehr and Nepstad 1994).

## Controlling Escalation

If an emerging conflict is framed by the opposing parties as a coercive rather than cooperative process, it is bound to escalate. That was certainly the case with the sit-in movement. Once racial desegregation was defined as the clear goal of southern blacks – and once it became clear that for most southern whites racial segregation was a way of life for which they would fight – cooperative resolution became only a dim possibility. And once military force had been used in the ethnically disputed sections of Croatia and Bosnia, the conflict escalated uncontrollably. As escalation occurs, however, it may become so costly that ways of moderating it will come into play. The idea, of course, is to bring those moderating methods to bear earlier rather than later, thereby reducing harmful consequences.

Although some conflicts can be controlled by addressing their underlying causes, such as unjust power distribution, and although some can be cooperatively resolved at relatively low cost, many inevitably escalate to higher levels of intensity and cost. Uncontrolled escalation is really something like cancer in the human body. Three approaches can control such escalation: getting adversaries to change their power strategies; introducing third-party intervention such as mediation; and using escalation methods that are self-limiting.

The reader should note that many of the specific approaches discussed here are a variation on the tit-for-tat strategy we considered in Chapter 7. Remember that this strategy recommends not only that each party should reciprocate the cooperative moves of the opponent (such as concessions) and his or her coercive moves (such as threats), but also that it should, at times, unilaterally make cooperative moves (such as breaking the deadlock).

### *Power Strategies*

Often, adversaries are reluctant to deescalate a conflict. They cling doggedly and irrationally to power strategies that are increasingly costly and even self-defeating. But not all power strategies involve the use of force, and there are ways of getting conflict parties to shift toward less costly power applications.

Boulding (1989) discusses three types of power: threat power, trading power, and giving power.[5] Threat power amounts to saying, "If you do something bad to me, I will do something as bad or worse to you." Even some forms of nonviolent direct action – such as strikes and boycotts – are threat-based. By contrast, exchange power suggests, "If you do something nice for me, I will reciprocate." Force is replaced with trade; the power contest gives way to negotiation. Further still from the use of force by a conflict party is unilateral giving power. It is reflected in the attitude, "I will do something nice for you simply because you are a fellow human being," or a decent person, or someone in need, or whatever. At the threat end of the power spectrum lies the "do to you" behavior. At the integrative or giving end is the no-strings-attached "do for you" action.

Force is a form of conflict behavior that should be used cautiously if at all. As a coercive action, it moves a conflict away from cooperative resolution. It also tends to be more costly to both the users and their opponents. The more costs that the adversaries sink into a conflict, the more difficult it is for them to write off the cost and shift to cooperative resolution. Even if force is not actually used by conflict parties, the possibility that they might use it will influence the conflict. Still, potential force is usually more useful for cooperative resolution than applied force. Because less harm is done, less needs to be undone later. We can think of threat as a moderate type of force.

In any conflict, a mix of the three types of power can be used. Shifting a conflict from a coercive mode to a cooperative resolution path requires that each party expand its trading and giving strategies and diminish its use of force or threat of force. Organizations and professional intervenor roles can be created to assist adversaries to make that shift, as was the case with the various civil wars in Central America in the 1980s. In that instance, mediators were particularly important in helping adversaries to change their power mixes toward deescalation.

The movement for civil rights in the United States illustrates how changing one's power strategy can increase the cost of conflict. Until the mid-1960s, civil rights leaders used a power mix of nonviolent force tempered with an integrative view of their opponents as fellow humans who were simply doing wrong. They also used some trading behavior in negotiations with businesses and governments in different cities throughout the South. That was a difficult power mix to sustain. It had to be forceful enough to open up segregated facilities yet sufficiently moderate to deter the full fury of racial backlash from southern whites. Nonviolent force was necessary to escalate the conflict, but nonviolent ideological restraint was required to prevent an explosive escalation.

Martin Luther King and other leaders of the Southern Christian Leadership Conference (SCLC) were able to maintain the more moderate mix into the mid-1960s, despite Black Panther and Student Nonviolent Coordinating Committee (SNCC) shifts toward increasingly militant strategies and the eruption of northern urban riots. But ultimately, SCLC rhetoric and tactics became more militant in an effort to retain control of the movement as it moved northward. When King was assassinated in 1968, the movement's radical wing ignored trading and giving power and went toe-to-toe with its opponents in urban police departments. That shift in power strategies was very costly for them and society generally.

The Nicaraguan civil war in the 1980s illustrates the opposite tendency, the way opposing sides reduce conflict costs by shifting away from threat-heavy power mixes to more cooperative ones (Wehr and Nepstad 1994). The Sandinista government was in conflict both with U.S.-supported Contra forces in the north and south and with indigenous groups on the Atlantic Coast. From middecade on, these opponents were increasingly persuaded by diplomats and by changing regional and global contexts to alter their strategy mixes toward cooperative resolution. Cease-fires were arranged and exchange behavior increased, with threats being increasingly replaced by cooperation. Integrative behavior expanded as negotiated agreements were implemented. Regional autonomy and subsequent reconciliation were worked out with the Atlantic Coast peoples. National elections were agreed to and resulted in a peaceful transfer of power in 1990 and a subsequent uneasy mutual tolerance among former adversaries.

A moderating shift in participants' power mixes occurred largely in response to the political context of the conflict. Some aspects of that context within Nicaragua itself were especially influential, notably the moderating influence of religious organizations and women in the Sandinista revolution. Changes in the global political context were also important: the Cold War was winding down, thus reducing the U.S.-Soviet military confrontation in Central America. Perhaps most important was the changing Central American context, where regional leaders had created the Esquipulas process and structure for resolving civil wars throughout the region. Opposing sides in Nicaragua used Esquipulas to expand their trading and integrating interaction with one another.

### Third-Party Interventions

We discuss intervention here rather than earlier in the chapter because intervenors such as mediators are usually not invited into a conflict until it is spiraling upward. When impartial third parties intervene in a conflict, new relational structures and possibilities for moderating the conflict are created. Introduction of a mediator, for example, changes the conflict's physical and social character, generating new intergroup relations and transactions. The presence of an observer tends to put contenders on better, if not their best, behavior. Intermediaries facilitate accurate communication, clarifying the contenders' issues, interests, and needs. They may even divert blame toward themselves as a technique for transforming stalemate into resolution. Most important, third parties bring additional minds and problem-solving skills to the conflict. The contenders are no longer on their own.

*Mediation.* A common type of intervention is mediation, best defined as negotiation facilitated by third, presumably impartial, parties. It is a rather formal process with certain stages that most mediators generally follow (Moore 1986). The third party assists the disputants to reframe their conflict, develop an agreement, and implement it. Usually, a mediator gets the conflict parties to reframe the dispute as a problem to be solved collaboratively, prepares an agreement signed by all three, and often guarantees its implementation. As a conflict emerges, the relationships of contending parties with one another take on a special character. Attention comes to focus ever more on the behavior of the adversary to the exclusion of any noncontenders involved. One justifies one's behavior increasingly by what the other has done rather than by any universal standard of correct behavior. A process Coleman (1957) has called reciprocal causation takes over so that each contender comes to form something like an independent social unit engrossed in tit-for-tat attack and defense behavior.[6] Without some external intervention, such dynamics can lead to extreme force being used at higher and higher cost.

Introduction of an impartial third party may moderate conflict because, as Porter and Taplin (1987) have noted, it transforms a two-party relationship into a three-party group, which creates a new relational system with new dynamics of communication, emotional responses, and conflict behavior. The third party becomes an observer, evaluator, and facilitator of the disputants' behavior, which they are likely to moderate accordingly. The new triadic system of relationships helps resolve the conflict in several ways: it stimulates disputant cooperation, permits face-saving, and provides for tension release.

Most important, the mediator gets the participants to reframe their reality. As we have already seen, many conflicts are largely a clash of different realities, mistakenly viewed by the opposing parties as objective facts. If a conflict is based on reality constructed by the opponents, it can just as well be reconstructed and reshaped by them into a less costly, more productive form.

Because the behavior of the mediator is of paramount importance, the effectiveness of various techniques and the relationship between a mediator and the disputants are topics much discussed by professional mediators. For example, are the most effective mediators those totally unconnected personally to the conflict parties and thus more impartial, as is generally believed? Or is connectedness with the conflict parties a useful mediator attribute, particularly in non-Western cultures (Wehr and Lederach 1991)? Some research suggests that mediators who are more sociable and empathic with the disputants in their personal style produce more agreements than those who remain distant from them (Bartos 1989).

Professional mediators differ in their philosophies. Some see their responsibility as simply to facilitate an agreement that the conflict parties agree is fair and workable. Although most mediators adhere to an impartiality principle, feeling that any favoring of one side over another destroys their usefulness, some believe that the mediation process should empower any party that is at an unfair disadvantage. Still others practice what is called "transformative mediation," where the intervening third party intends not only to reach agreement but to modify the conflict relationship and setting (Busch and Folger 1994).

*Intermediation.* In the intervention approach known as "intermediation," an intermediary plays a quite different role than the formal mediator whose role we have just described. The intermediaries work to facilitate communication between conflicting parties. Their involvement normally extends over long periods and is particularly useful in very sensitive and potentially explosive conflicts. They function, for example, as conveyers of information between heads of state or hostile ethnic communities who cannot be seen by their constituents to have contact with the "enemy." Once fully trusted by the opposing sides, they sometimes suggest gestures or unilateral concessions that might lead to a lessening of tension and to negotiation. They must generally be superb communicators and confidants (Kolb 1995). Total impartiality is important. That is why Quaker conciliators, with their reputation for being able to see truth on all sides, have often succeeded as intermediaries where others have failed (Yarrow 1978).

On occasion, several methods will be used in the same conflict. One of the authors of the present work was asked to help resolve a difficult conflict within a university physics department. There were actually two types of conflict going on: conflict between project groups over space and equipment, and conflict due to extreme tension between the leaders of those groups. The mediator used a multitrack approach. First, he interviewed each of the ten participants to "map" a shared reality of the conflict and locate some ideas for resolving it. He also reduced the leaders' hostility through face-to-face mediation with them. Finally, he used a "single text agreement technique," circulating three successive draft agreements until one acceptable to all was achieved. All participants claimed ownership of the settlement at a signing ceremony that ended with a champagne toast. Five years later, the agreed-upon arrangement continued to work reasonably well.

*Multimodal Intermediation.* Many types of third parties can be introduced into a conflict, working together either simultaneously or at different points when their form of assistance is most needed. There are many different functions intermediaries can perform. Intervention may begin with the "explorer," who assures the contenders that the other side's goal is not total victory, and end with the "reconciler," who facilitates the healing process (Mitchell 1993). Along the path of resolution, unifiers, facilitators, legitimators, and many other specialists may be introduced. Such a multimodal approach is especially useful with large-scale conflicts. An intervention team must use its skills and relationships with the contenders at the right time, in the right context. Even intraorganizational and two-person conflict could benefit from the team approach, though the types of intervenors would be fewer. Who is there who could help us out of this conflict? This should be the first question conflict opponents should ask. The more varied their concept of third parties, the more intermediary potential they will see as they look around them.

The multiplicity of intermediary roles and functions has been illustrated in numerous contemporary international conflicts (Miall et al. 1999). Efforts to end civil war in Bosnia suggest many of them: involvement of European Community representatives as intermediaries and mediators (though these plans mostly failed); United Nations humanitarian peace keeping, involving modest military, medical, and supply forces to protect major urban centers; NATO military interposition to implement the Dayton Agreement and support political reconstruction; and citizen reconciliation teams from nongovernmental organizations.

In the Nicaraguan civil war, intermediation was done in a number of ways (Wehr and Lederach 1991). Within the Esquipulas process, the presidents of the Central American nations created conciliation commissions for each of the civil wars in progress. Oscar Arias, president of Costa Rica, played the lead intermediary role, because his nation has been historically neutral and unarmed since 1948. His persuasive intervention got the Sandinista government and its opponents to agree to demilitarize the conflict and hold meaningful elections.

A second conflict, between the Sandinistas and Atlantic Coast indigenous groups, complicated Nicaraguan peacemaking. Intermediary types essential in that process included insider-partial mediators such as Cardinal Obando y Bravo and outsider-neutral mediators such as Jimmy Carter. International observer teams monitored the elections and the subsequent transfer of power. Reconciliation teams have now been working nearly a decade to reintegrate demobilized soldiers from both sides into their towns and villages.

*Interposition.* Another approach to controlling escalation is the placing of a neutral third party physically between the conflicting parties. At the international level, multinational peace keeping has for forty years been a common way of preventing conflict and violence. Military forces and observers are interposed between opposing sides. As Yugoslavia was coming apart in the early 1990s, a new variant of peace keeping was tried, preventive deployment (Carnegie 1997, 64). Macedonia, intending to become an independent state, was threatened with attack from Serbia. A United Nations military and political contingent, sent to Macedonia as a deterrent, has also played an intermediary role between the Macedonian and Serbian governments.

A preventive presence of third parties need not be military or governmental. Increasingly, private citizens groups have intervened to prevent violence (Wehr 1996). In the Nicaraguan civil war of the 1980s, international teams from Witness for Peace were stationed along Nicaragua's borders and in strategic villages at high risk of Contra attack (Griffin-Nolan 1991). The assumption underlying such a practice is that the presence of unarmed foreigners deters attacks on civilians in war zones. The same principle underlies international accompaniment (Mahony and Eguren 1997), where foreign observers stay with human rights leaders whose protest work puts them at risk in civil conflicts. The deployment of two thousand civilian human rights monitors in the Kosovo province of Yugoslavia through the Organization for Cooperation and Security in Europe is an interesting recent example. United Nations peace-keeping forces have often been deployed in civil conflicts, with varying success (Carnegie 1997).

Organizations such as corporations, universities, and school systems have created ombuds staff who interpose themselves in internal disputes. Ironically, the very hierarchical structures that have embraced such cooperative mechanisms may shy away from using them effectively. The university conflict described in Chapter 6 is a case in point: although both the faculty and the administration incurred extremely high costs, neither would use ombuds staff as intermediaries.

### Unilateral Deescalation

Interrupting and reversing the escalatory spiral is at the heart of conflict moderation. One approach is known as GRIT (graduated reciprocation in tension reduction; Osgood 1962). One side interrupts the upward spiral by taking a modest unilateral step to halt it, either by declining to reciprocate the opponent's last move or by actually moving back down the spiral. The initiator waits for expected reciprocation by the other side.

Patfoort (1995) presents escalation not as a spiral but as a ratcheting process in which parties alternate in trying to maintain dominance in their relationship. Each climb-up requires a more forceful and aggressive action than before. Father-son conflict often assumes such a major-minor pattern. A zigzag effect rather than a spiral is produced. This dynamic is interrupted unilaterally when the dominated party refuses to remain in the low-power position but declines to rise above one of simple equivalence with the adversary.

*Self-Limiting Escalation.* Some kinds of escalation have a built-in limitation (Wehr 1979). The Gandhian method of satyagraha, active noncooperation of one party to escape domination by another, is a good illustration. By its ideological restraint and its controlled approach to escalation, satyagraha holds in check the "runaway responses" that Coleman (1957) identifies as prime motivators of uncontrolled escalation: generalization of issues, shift from disagreement to antagonism, information distortion, tit-for-tat symmetry (without unilateral concessions),[7] and extremist leadership. Although an ideological commitment to nonviolence was certainly the most important element controlling escalation in Gandhi's satyagaha campaigns, his other strategic and tactical policies also inhibited runaway escalation. Take, for example, his stepwise method of escalating confrontation in a campaign: he would end each campaign episode by withdrawing with his lieutenants to an ashram for a period of reflection and meditation, further communication with his opponents, and manual labor. This hiatus permitted a wiser – more rational – decision about the next upward step to be taken.[8] At any of these intervals of reflection and withdrawal between escalating steps, the challenger might suspend confrontation, return to less intense levels of conflict, and reopen negotiation with the opponent. A similar possibility for suspending a power contest to reopen negotiation is built into the contemporary approach known as dispute system design ( Ury et al. 1993). Looping back to negotiation as integral to one's way of doing conflict is a powerful conflict-moderating device.

Gandhi's way of dealing with conflict had another moderating aspect. He viewed his opponents as partners in a search for truth. Bondurant (1988) has conceptualized satyagraha as the "Gandhian Dialectic"; nonviolent action (antithesis) engages established structures of power (thesis) in a truth-seeking struggle leading to a more just and truthful relationship between the parties in conflict (synthesis). That was very much the way Martin Luther King approached the civil rights struggle in the United States. So while such conflict approaches may appear coercive to the casual observer, they have important cooperative "partnership in problem solving" elements as well.

## Conclusions

Conflict-moderating approaches tend to have a synergistic effect when applied together. Bosnian peacemaking illustrates how the moderating approaches we have discussed in this chapter can be complementarily applied. It took a long process of intermediation, mediation, and negotiation before the 1995 Dayton Agreement was reached. To reach it, reluctant leaders had to be brought to the table, and threat strategies – including military force and economic sanctions – had to be used by third parties such as NATO and the European Community. The linchpin of the agreement's implementation was interposition of multinational military forces to separate the opposing sides: an initial intervention force superseded by a stabilization force, which remains in place at this writing. This enforced separation of the three sides permitted the building of institutions for resolving residual conflict and encouraging reconciliation, particularly within multiethnic villages where those could be reestablished (Murray 1997).

In these pages, we have presented a number of theories of conflict processes, illustrative real-world applications, and methods for dealing with conflict creatively and at reasonable cost. In a sense, we all are conflict actors most of the time, working at the craft of getting along with others, meeting our needs and defending our interests, minimizing harm to others and society. Human experience has provided us with a substantial number of tools to handle conflict well. We must learn to use these tools skillfully, judging wisely when to use which approaches under what circumstances and in which settings. Escalation is sometimes necessary, but when? Negotiation is often mutually beneficial for all parties, but not always so. Even force is sometimes called for to protect life and other things of value, but is it physical or intimidating force that is required? We must constantly be asking ourselves, Which tools work well together and which do not? When and for how long should they be used? Perhaps most important, our choice of conflict action methods should be informed by our accumulated theoretical understanding of how conflict works.

The secret to preventing the escalation of costly conflict is really not a secret at all. As we noted in Chapter 1, for at least two centuries now humans have been consciously learning how to do so and have practiced it and reflected upon it. Were our efforts not hampered by the breakneck speed with which weapons are developed, and the pressures of rapid population growth, we would probably have resolved the problem already. We must continue to train ever larger numbers of individuals and groups in how to manage conflict more economically.

Although human knowledge about conflict increased substantially in the twentieth century, so has the world's population and the technology of violence. In this new century and millennium, conflict actors must increasingly practice the "principles of good conflict": clarifying goals and interests to move coercive conflict toward cooperative resolution; selecting conflict strategies and tactics rationally and applying them economically to further those interests; and using conflict knowledge to inform our practice of conflict as we reduce its cost.

# CHAPTER TEN

# Understanding and Managing Conflicts

IN THIS FINAL chapter, we review the most important principles and methods of understanding and managing conflicts, then suggest how conflict students might use them in building their personal and professional lives. Whether these insights are valuable to you is, of course, for you to decide. But you will probably agree that you *did* learn something new. But what exactly was it? Let's go over the main points.

## Understanding Conflicts

You may feel that exact definitions are, by and large, a waste of time. We agree, but only up to a point: there are a few basic concepts that you really ought to know. The concept of conflict is one of them.

### Conflict

You may recall that, in Chapter 2, we defined conflict as a situation in which *actors use conflict behavior against each other to attain incompatible goals and/or express their hostility*. Chances are that this definition, when you first encountered it, did not mean much. But it should mean more now that you have explored, in depth, the meaning of the three main concepts in that definition: conflict behavior, incompatible goals, and hostility.

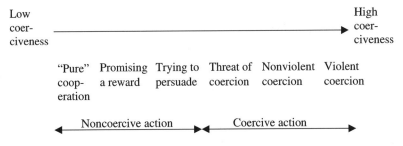

**Figure 10.1.** Coerciveness of Conflict Action

Perhaps you remember that "conflict behavior" can be viewed both as a set of categories and as a continuum. We distinguished two main categories of conflict behavior, noncoercive (which includes pure co-operation, promising reward, and persuasion) and coercive (which includes threat of coercion, nonviolent coercion, and violent coercion). And we noted that, as shown in Figure 10.1, these distinct types of behavior can be arranged on a continuum of increasing coerciveness. You should also recall that, whenever possible, we agreed to speak about conflict *action* (rather than conflict behavior). The reasons for this were given in Chapter 2.

The main point to remember about "incompatible goals" is that they can best be represented through payoff matrices. For example, the goals of some imaginary factory workers and their managers can be represented by a payoff matrix shown in Table 10.1. Although this table represents the goals in an oversimplified manner, it does provide you with a new way of thinking about incompatibility.

First, it shows what the *goals* of the actors are. Consider, for example, the goals of the workers. As you may recall, to find them you need to identify the rows that have a *positive* payoff for them. (Table 10.1 shows that the first and third rows qualify.) And the *labels* of these rows tell you what worker's goals are (the wage of $20, and the solvency of the firm). Second, you can find for any two goals whether they are compatible or incompatible for the two sides: if both adversaries have positive payoffs from them, then those goals are compatible; otherwise they are incompatible. (Thus the goals of $20 wage and $10 wage are incompatible.)

Table 10.1. *Compatible and Incompatible Goals of Workers and Managers*

|  | Conflict Parties | |
|---|---|---|
|  | Workers | Managers |
| *Goals* | | |
| Wage: $20 per hour | 7 | −3 |
| Wage: $10 per hour | −4 | 8 |
| Solvency of the firm | 2 | 5 |

Now for the last concept in our definition of conflict, "hostility." The main thing to remember is that hostility is best seen as nonrational behavior, one that occurs without the benefit of careful – and usually prolonged – deliberation. Hostility-driven behavior tends to start and end abruptly, to be violent, and not to benefit either actor. At the same time, hostile *feelings* can have consequences that are useful to an actor: as Figure 5.2 shows, they contribute to group solidarity and thus increase that group's power. Still, this advantage may be offset by costs. Recall that while the aggressive action of minority faculty and students helped a Chicano professor to get his tenure, it left many faculty members alienated and doubtful of the award's validity (see Chapter 6).

### Causes of Conflict

No doubt, one's reluctance to spend too much time on definitions stems from the desire to get quickly to the heart of the matter and find why conflicts occur. What causes them? Is there one main reason, or are there many? How can I explain this *particular* conflict, one that I am concerned with?

These are all good and important concerns. And yet, before we addressed them, we had to take one more stab at conceptualization. This was because questions such as, Why did this conflict happen? are inherently ambiguous. Are we asking about the hidden causes that created goal incompatibility over a long period of time, without ever erupting into an open conflict? Or do we wish to know why these hidden problems suddenly broke into the open? Or do we wish to know why, once on its way, the conflict has been escalating?

These questions suggest that we should distinguish between three main sets of causes: those that lead to goal incompatibility,[1] those that lead to the beginning of open fighting, and those that promote escalation. You may wish to think of these three sets of causes as defining three consecutive stages of a conflict – seeing the "latent" conflict during which incompatible goals are identified as the first stage; the onset of open fighting as the second stage; and the ensuing escalation as the third stage. If this is helpful, by all means see conflict in that way. But do not forget that a given cause may keep on working past "its" stage. For example, the events that, in the distant past, created a sense of injustice and thus contributed to goal incompatibility may continue to work as grievances that contribute to the outbreak of open fighting and, ultimately, to escalation.

Recall that the "root" causes of conflicts – the causes of *goal incompatibility* – were of considerable interest to classical theoreticians, and that they found quite a few of them. Our theory, summarized in Figure 3.2, takes most of them into account. We shall not discuss them again at this point; if you wish to refresh your memory, please read again Chapter 3 (in which the theory is described) and Chapter 4 (in which it is applied to the civil rights struggle). Suffice it to say here that we identified three main sources of goal incompatibility: contested resources, incompatible roles, and incompatible values.

These causes may be working for a long time without ever bringing the conflict to the surface. And yet they set the stage for it, so that if some additional factors enter the scene, *open* conflict is very likely to occur. As Figure 5.2 shows, open conflict is just around the corner when each side acquires high conflict solidarity and assembles the necessary conflict resources. At that point even a minor new grievance can become a "trigger event" – an event that starts open fighting. We showed in Chapter 6 how these causes were at work within a university setting and how a denial of tenure triggered bitter infighting.

You may recall our discussion of *escalation* (and deescalation) as something that made you uncomfortable, even anxious. This was because we began to use mathematical equations. But remember why we did so at that point (in Chapter 7). True, we were able to go far without using mathematics. We maintained that Party's escalation is always driven by three main tendencies: to escalate unilaterally, to reciprocate (or, possibly, retaliate),[2] and to express hostility. We argued that the magnitude of these three escalatory tendencies was determined, to a large extent, by the same forces that brought about open conflict (see Figure 7.4). Finally, we listed several feedbacks from the conflict itself that could provide further impetus to escalation (Figure 7.5) and deescalation (Figure 7.6).

But some questions could not be answered without using a mathematical model. Can escalation occur even when the "inner" escalatory tendencies (toward unilateral escalation, reciprocation, and hostility) remain unchanged? Under what conditions will the conflict settle to a steady (equilibrium) state? What will happen if only one side starts escalating or deescalating? Can stable peace be maintained when the former opponents remain hostile toward each other? You may wish to look again at Figures 7.1, 7.2, and 7.3, and read the discussion that explains them. You may further bolster your understanding by rereading our account of the Bosnian conflict (see Chapter 8).

### Dealing with Ongoing Conflicts

There are three main tools for dealing with an opponent in an ongoing conflict: overwhelming force, negotiation, and the tit-for-tat strategy. We discussed the first approach, the use of *overwhelming force*, in Chapter 7. There are many historical examples of its effectiveness. For example, when in the twelfth century Genghis Khan massacred the populations of cities he conquered, he terrified many opponents into submission; when during World War II the Nazis destroyed the town of Lidice, most of the Czech resistance against them stopped; when the United States dropped atomic bombs on two Japanese cities, the Japanese government soon capitulated.

But, as we also noted in Chapter 7, this strategy is flawed in several ways. Above all, the brutality required for its application is morally unacceptable today. Even in seemingly less drastic cases – such as when heavy bombing of Yugoslavia by NATO helped end the fighting in Kosovo – the public outcry against civilian casualties tends to make this strategy too costly to apply. Thus the remaining two strategies become increasingly appealing.

Most of us would agree that conflicts can be best managed through *negotiation* – and we discussed that process in detail in Chapter 9 and will return to it shortly. But our theory suggests that parties will refuse to negotiate whenever waging the conflict with force has higher payoff than does negotiation. Sometimes leaders' interests (payoffs) are furthered by continuing, even intensifying, a conflict. Even when leaders might wish to negotiate, they may be kept from doing so by popular attitudes. For example, the leaders in the Israeli-Palestinian conflict have often refused to negotiate because they feared that they would be swept from office if they did.

Thus one often has to consider a strategy that falls between the two extremes of force and compromise, such as the tit-for-tat strategy. As explained in Chapter 8, this strategy has two main components, reciprocation and unilateral deescalation. You reciprocate by matching the magnitude and severity of your opponent's escalation and deescalation. For example, when the United States expels several Russian diplomats for spying, Russia may expel the same number of U.S. diplomats; when Russia releases an American spy, the United States may release a Russian spy of equal importance. You can deescalate unilaterally by making a goodwill gesture. For example, you can help to resolve an ongoing battle with your spouse by giving her or him something of personal value – be it a handsome ring or bouquet of roses.

The mainstay of this third strategy is reciprocation. It calls for *equal* responses – something that may be hard to execute. On one hand, you may punish your opponent too severely. For example, when Palestinian youths began to throw rocks at Israeli troops, the Israelis opened fire, killing several of them. This response was too strong and thus invited further escalation from the Palestinians. (At the same time, it was not "extreme" enough to stop Palestinian resistance.) On the other hand, you may apply lesser sanctions than you should. For example, when Great Britain and France failed to respond to Hitler's aggression against the Ruhrland, Austria, and Czechoslovakia, Hitler became convinced that he could attack Poland without encountering Allied resistance as well. He was wrong, of course, and World War II resulted.

The tit-for-tat strategy is far from ideal. Unlike overwhelming force, it does not promise to bring capitulation of one's opponent; unlike negotiation, it does not promise to bring about lasting peace. What it does do is prevent the conflict from escalating. It may even encourage gradual deescalation, both because it prescribes occasional goodwill gestures and because it allows enough time for the conflict-reducing feedbacks to work.

## Becoming a Skilled Conflict Actor

For many readers, the real value of conflict theory is its practical usefulness in everyday life. Because social conflict is inherent in the social system, you encounter it often. And making it less harmful and more productive can be rewarding for you, the conflict student. If you want to know not only why a given conflict exists but also what to *do* about it, you might wish to reread Chapter 9. If, in addition, you wish to consider becoming a skilled conflict actor in both your personal and professional life, take the following four steps: become familiar with basic conflict theory and methods for applying it; learn to use theory-based methods in everyday life; undergo rigorous professional training; and familiarize yourself with conflict work in a number of professional fields to find the right career fit.

### *Learn the Theory and Methods for Applying It*

Because the principles of conflict theory can be used at any level, the first step might be to create a table that shows how certain theoretical principles suggest specific steps for reducing conflict harm and increasing productivity. Table 10.2 shows how the rules for constructing payoff matrices may help you to find the best course of action in any given conflict. It also shows that our theory can help you understand your opponents' coerciveness: what their goals are and why they hold them, and why they may be hostile toward you. It also suggests how you can use the feedbacks generated by the conflict to deescalate it.

### *Use These Methods in Everyday Life*

The best learning begins with practice in daily life and feedback on how well you are managing conflict. If you are interested in peacemaking as a profession, you might begin developing skills such as suggested in Table 10.2 and using them consciously and consistently in you relations with all those with whom you live and work.

Table 10.2. *Some Theory-Based Methods*

| Theoretical Principles | Resulting Methods |
| --- | --- |
| *Payoff Matrices* | |
| Rational decision making is facilitated by the use of payoff matrices: | Before you decide how to act, go through the following steps: |
| 1. Construct the matrix so that each row represents a viable option, each column a conflict actor. | 1. Write down *all* options available to you and your opponents. |
| 2. For each cell of the matrix, imagine the relevant outcome. | 2. For each option, write down *all* possible consequences. |
| 3. Assign payoff to each cell. | 3. Specify how you and your opponents feel about these consequences. (At the very least, write down "acceptable" or "not acceptable.") |
| 4. Choose the option that has the highest positive payoff for both actors. | 4. Search for the options that are acceptable to both you and your opponent. If several are acceptable, advocate the one that is best for both. If no option is acceptable to both, search for new options. Go back to step 2. |
| *Main Reasons for Coercive Behavior* | |
| Opponents may be coercive: | When trying to determine what options your opponents favor (steps 1–3 above), do the following: |
| 1. Their goals are incompatible with yours. | 1. Consider the reasons why your opponents' goals are different from yours: they might have been treated unjustly, may live in abject conditions, may be belligerent, may play a role that is incompatible with yours, or may have values that are incompatible with yours (see Table 3.1). |

Table 10.2. *(cont.)*

| Theoretical Principles | Resulting Methods |
|---|---|
| 2. They have formed a conflict group. | 2. Consider the reasons why the conflict groups developed, paying special attention to hostility-creating factors: the grievances the opponents might have against you, and the conditions that might have frustrated them (see Figure 5.2). |

*How to Use Feedback to Deescalate the Conflict*

| | |
|---|---|
| Opponents may be coercive: | Decrease opponents' coerciveness: |
| 1. The conflict generated certain feedbacks. | 1. Dampen the *escalatory* feedbacks by becoming less threatening and making amends for past transgressions (see Figure 7.5). |
| | 2. Encourage *dee*scalatory feedbacks. Show how the conflict has inflicted – and can continue to inflict – damage on both sides, such as depleted resources, personal losses, and loss of status (see Figure 7.6). |

Conceptually, you might place yourself at the center of life settings of increasing scale: home, friendship groups, workplace, community, wider world, and profession (see Figure 10.2). You could sharpen your conflict skills at all of these levels as you move outward toward a conflict career, locating yourself at the center of the conflict careers map, then imagining how you would use conflict theory and method at each level. Some theorists and practitioners maintain that "peacemaking begins at home" and that one who would use positive conflict skills in his or her professional life must develop them first at home with siblings, children, adolescents, and spouses (Patfoort 2001).

### Undergo Rigorous Professional Training

In recent decades conflict training programs have grown in many shapes and sizes around the world (See Table 10.3). They range from

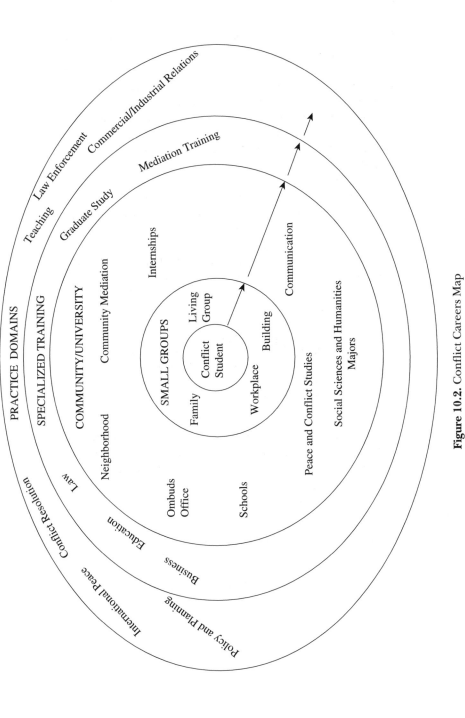

**Figure 10.2.** Conflict Careers Map

Table 10.3. *Specialized Training: Where Conflict Professionals Learn*

---

*Graduate Study:* Conflict Resolution: Inderdisciplinary programs are described in the *COPRED Global Directory* and at websites such as <www.crinfo.org>, and <www.csf.colorado.edu/peace>. Such programs would include Notre Dame's Kroc Institute <www.nd.edu/~krocinst>, George Mason's Institute for Conflict Analysis and Resolution <www.gmu.edu/departments/ICAR>, University of Bradford's Peace Studies Program <www.bradford.ac.uk>, and the European University <www.aspr.ac.at>.

> *Social Sciences:* Sociology, psychology and anthropology are the most likely to have association sections and journals on conflict analysis and peacemaking. Their graduate training can lead to conflict management teaching and practice in many professional fields.
>
> *Policy Sciences:* These graduates generally find their way into policy planning and implementation positions where resolving conflicts over environmental impacts, water resources, and social problems will be a major part of their work.

*Education:* Educators are increasingly being trained to be peacemakers in their schools, communities, and universities. Lesley University <www.lesley.edu>, for example, offers a "Peaceable Schools" degree focusing on intraschool conflict management. Peer mediation, ombuds offices, and funding conflicts are all receiving the attention of teaching professionals, as the Conflict Resolution in Education website suggests <www.CRENet.org>.

*Mediation Training:* There are hundreds of community-level programs in North America and a growing number in Europe as well. Many of these offer certificates with specialization in different conflict types. Some, <cdr@mediate.org>, even send trainers to other nations. A directory of organizations at all levels is now being developed at <www.crinfo.org/v2-educ-train.cfm>.

*Law and Business:* Many law schools now have at least an emphasis in Alternative Dispute Resolution as reflected in the American Bar Association <www.abanet.org/dispute/home.html>. Most business schools teach the theory and practice of negotiation, bargaining , mediation, and arbitration.

---

community mediation programs that prepare volunteers to serve their neighborhoods to university programs in conflict management whose graduates go on to university teaching and international service with nongovernmental organizations specializing in humanitarian relief and civil society rehabilitation. Somewhere near 450 academic programs in peace and conflict studies now exist at the university level around the world, ranging from several courses to full degree programs. More than half of these programs contain words (e.g., conflict or dispute resolution; diplomacy, peacemaking, mediation, or negotiation) suggesting an impressive array of conflict training opportunities around the globe (*COPRED* 2000).

### *Familiarize Yourself with Many Professional Fields*

The final stage on the pathway is getting to know the various professional fields where conflict knowledge is valued and sought after. Interest in conflict management and transformation has expanded so rapidly in the past decade that one can no longer know it all. Of course, the formal training stage will familiarize the conflict student with what is out there. But increasingly, conflict practitioners travel across professional fields because the same theory and method, coming more and more from the same conflict knowledge pool, can be used everywhere. And the conflict intervenor roles are rapidly multiplying as we better understand the complexity of the really tough conflicts.[3] The Internet has become an invaluable tool for finding one's way around. Table 10.4 briefly describes professional fields where conflict skills are highly valued and frequently used. Only space limitations constrain the number of websites listed here that can lead conflict students around the peacemaking profession.

## Routes to Careers

The routes by which conflict students work their way out from their immediate life settings at the center of the career map to the professions on the perimeter are as numerous as those finding their way. For example, student A might be especially interested in teaching about and managing conflict among adolescents. A's pathway might be through an undergraduate peace or conflict studies program, then to graduate

Table 10.4. *Practice Domains: Where Conflict Professionals Work*

---

*Conflict Resolution:* This field encompasses conflict management specialists in education, family mediation, intraorganizational disputes and conflict resolution – in other words, any professional making a living primarily at resolving conflict. The Association for Conflict Resolution website <www.spidr.org/> suggests for the reader the field's diversity and career possibilities.

*International Peace Development:* This field has grown especially rapidly in the 1980s and 1990s, as governments, and intergovernmental and nongovernmental organizations have responded to civil conflicts around the world. Whether one is a refugee relief worker, a human rights advocate, a civilian monitor for elections or peace keeping, a diplomat, a conflict transformation trainer, a physician, or a sustainable agriculture specialist working in conflict areas, conflict management skills, used particularly across ethnic and linguistic lines and in situations of crisis, are essential. Several good sources on such work are available at Conciliation Resources <www.c-r.org>; Organization for Security and Cooperation in Europe <www.osce.org>; United Nations <www.un.org>.

*Public Policy:* As population grows and shifts, and resources diminish, policy officials encounter more and more conflict. Consultation among stakeholders requires increasing conflict skill from planners. Enforcement of government regulation and standards produces more and more citizen versus government friction and developer versus government tension. Urban governments have resident conflict specialists or hire them when needed.

*Commercial or Industrial Peacemaking:* Labor-management mediation, conflict management within firms, and consumer arbitration provide a limitless need for conflict professionals here. See <www.adr.org/>.

---

study in education, specializing in peer mediation and violence reduction. With the degree in hand, student A may locate a position through the National Association for Mediation in Education or the Society for Professionals in Dispute Resolution. If not, student A may create his own program, such as the Colorado School Mediation Project.

Student B is a history major who goes on to graduate study in conflict sociology. Her special interest is in peace and human rights movements. After she completes her doctorate and a postdoctoral fellowship at Princeton, she is hired to direct a conflict studies program at a major university. Her writing is required reading in scores of social movement courses and activist organizations (Nepstad 1997; 2001).

Student C begins as a major in peace studies and math at a small Midwestern liberal arts college, works with a Mennonite conciliation service, goes on to earn a Ph.D. in sociology, writing his dissertation in Central America while working as a mediator in the Nicaraguan civil war. He goes on to found a university program in conflict transformation where he combines teaching, training middle-level leaders in civil conflicts from Somalia, to Guatemala, to Northern Ireland, and writing (Lederach 1997; 1999).

Student D studies international relations and minors in peace studies as an undergraduate. After earning an M.A. in peace studies at Notre Dame he spends two years in Panama with the Peace Corps returning to the United States fluent in Spanish and with a deeper understanding of conflict and the developing world. He takes a doctorate in sociology as he writes and teaches about social activism (Jones et al. 2001).

Students E and F receive Ph.D.s in conflict sociology, go on to postdoctoral fellowships at MIT, work in environmental dispute resolution, and build a global conflict resolution information network (Burgess and Burgess 1997).

We know of these particular pathways to conflict careers because the people following them are our former students, not imaginary creations. Students in other disciplines are taking equally interesting paths. We should emphasize again, however, the need to be learning those conflict skills in practice in everyday life in conjunction with more formal training.

Understanding how social conflict works and how to deal with it less harmfully and more productively can lead students of conflict to more meaningful professional and private lives. Conflict knowledge has a bright future, as do those who study and learn to use it effectively.

# Prelude to the Dissolution of Yugoslavia

THE PROGRESSIVE disintegration of Yugoslavia from 1991 onward can be seen as one part of the larger process of political reorganization in Soviet bloc nations, begun by the Polish Solidarity movement in 1980 (Wehr 1985). The winds of change were blowing into every corner of central and eastern Europe. But Yugoslavia, as a Communist state long independent of the Soviet Union, had an unusual set of factors variously restraining and stimulating conflict among its republics and ethnic communities.

## The Early Stage

Yugoslavia had become a nation-state – a constitutional monarchy – only at the end of World War I. Until then, the region had been an uneasy frontier among the Austro-Hungarian, Russian, and Ottoman empires. Each empire had used its coreligionists in the area – Croatian Catholics, Serbian Orthodox, and Muslims – to further its imperial aims. In fact, the assassination of Austro-Hungarian archduke Ferdinand in 1914 by a Serbian nationalist in Sarajevo provided the flashpoint for World War I.

Between the world wars, Yugoslavia's fragile nationhood was held hostage by nascent Croatian and Serbian nationalism. But Yugoslav communism and the political nationalism forming around Tito during

World War II provided an integrating force countering any tendencies toward ethnic separation. Tito, a Moscow-trained operative whose real name was Josip Broz, emerged as the leader of antifascist forces and became a legendary hero – the first real embodiment of Yugoslav nationalism. With massive popular support, his Yugoslav Communist Party easily assumed control of postwar Yugoslavia.

Tito's dream of a unified Yugoslavia took the form of a socialist federal state of six republics and two autonomous regions, and with a national government seated in Belgrade, the capital of the former royal Yugoslavia. Tito's stature as a war hero and his considerable political acumen provided the glue that, until his death in 1980, held Yugoslavia together. He sought to govern by leading rather than controlling. He believed that a federal Yugoslavia could survive only if sufficient political and economic resources were redistributed among the republics and away from Belgrade. Thus the national government shifted some of its economic development support away from the already somewhat industrialized northern republics of Slovenia and Croatia toward the south, which was still relatively rural – Serbia, Montenegro, Macedonia, and especially Bosnia. This redistribution occurred within the larger process of socialist industrial planning. Industrialization in Yugoslavia, as elsewhere in socialist Europe, was to be the engine of economic growth. The redistribution, while naturally not popular in the north, reinforced Yugoslav nationalism, particularly in Bosnia.

Postwar reconstruction and modernization were accomplished in part with development projects undertaken throughout Yugoslavia. They were supported financially by the United Nations and aided by enthusiastic volunteer youth brigades organized by the Communist Party of Yugoslavia (CPY). Despite widespread devastation, these efforts succeeded by the end of 1946 in bringing productivity back to prewar levels. Roads, bridges, and railway lines were repaired and rebuilt, factories were restored to working order, and power facilities were reconstructed (Donia and Fine 1994, 165).

These projects continued throughout Yugoslavia well into the 1960s. One of the present authors remembers working there as a work camper in 1958 and 1964 on highway and youth center construction. Youth from different Yugoslav republics lived, worked, and played together in these summer projects. They wore simple khaki uniforms and were organized into "brigades." Excursions took them to Tito's partisan headquarters in the mountains and to his village birthplace. They spent their evenings playing, dancing, and singing the music of Yugoslavia's different nationalities around large bonfires. Work was physical and unifying.

National economic recovery was certainly the manifest purpose of these projects. But equally significant was their latent function – bringing together youth volunteers from the different republics and ethnic traditions for political and cultural experience as Yugoslavs. The sense of a new national spirit pervading these projects seemed to eclipse narrower allegiances while celebrating the ties of ethnicity, religion, and region that the volunteers brought with them. Those more limited national identities were being skillfully woven into the fabric of a larger nationalism. At the time, it seemed that this new Yugoslav nationalism might take permanent root.

We should note here that Yugoslavia eventually dissolved in the 1990s primarily because of larger social, economic, and political forces, not so much because of any tradition of explosive interethnic antipathy, a myth planted in the world's public mind by the popular media. True, once the process of disintegration had begun, regional political leaders used those larger forces to stimulate ethnic fears and suspicions to use for personal gain. But the larger forces, very strong indeed, had created the context for them: Tito's failure to build alternative national bases for political mobilization; an economic decline, as Germany reduced its need for Yugoslav workers, and the Soviets reduced economic support; repayment of postwar loans coming due; and the general dissolution of socialist Europe.

Forces of decentralization had also been developing for decades. In 1948, Yugoslavia, unwilling to submit to Soviet political and economic hegemony, was expelled from the Cominform. It forged ahead with its own experiment in independent communism. Industrialization was emphasized, but the Soviet central planning model was discarded in favor of worker self-management, a sort of democratic workplace socialism. The workers in each enterprise hired and fired their managers, set production goals and worker benefits, found markets for their products, and generally ran their workplaces. While defying Stalin and creating a purely Yugoslav economic model did strengthen national

(Yugoslav) unity, over time that model encouraged decentralization and regional loyalty.

Other policies also encouraged a loosening of federal ties and unitary politics. For example, in the 1950s the Communist Party was reorganized: the national party was renamed the League of Communists of Yugoslavia, and the communist parties of the various republics became more powerful in relation to the political center in Serbia (Donia and Fine 1994, 171). Those strengthened parties were later used by ethnic and nationalist leaders to further their personal power ambitions and to favor the individual republics' interests over national ones. These trends were supported by the political theory of Tito's Slovenian associate, Edvard Kardelj, who had developed the concept of worker self-management. Kardelj urged that Yugoslav state nationalism was not to be forced upon the people in order to displace their various ethnic and regional allegiances, but rather was to subsume those loyalties, embrace them, and celebrate them. The Yugoslav model, then, largely reflected his thinking.

Tito's reputation of mythic proportions, his personal charisma, and his considerable political skill managed to sustain a federal, unified Yugoslavia for nearly forty years. As great leaders often do, however, Tito failed to provide for an orderly succession of leadership. He continually fragmented those concentrations of power that might successfully govern after him and hold Yugoslavia together. Kardelj was the only leader with sufficient national stature to have successfully succeeded Tito. Had he lived longer, he might have been able to hold the nation together, at least for a few more years.

Tito the pragmatist and Kardelj the theorist together embodied the Yugoslav nation as a political, economic, and cultural unit. They left the political scene more or less together, and thus set the stage for the next act, the steady deterioration of federal unity, and decreasing restraint on regionalism and ethnic chauvinism.

Tito and his Yugoslav nationalism had always been more popular in Bosnia than in any of the other republics, because Bosnians had benefited most from Belgrade's economic redistribution policies. Muslim Bosnians in particular supported Yugoslav nationalism, because, unlike Serbs and Croats in Bosnia, they had no ethnic ties to other republics. Their allegiance to the nation-state was reflected in the

1953 national census, when Bosnian Muslims identified themselves as Yugoslavs, while Bosnian Croats and Serbs identified themselves almost exclusively as members of their ethnic communities (Donia and Fine 1994, 177). By the 1980s there had been considerable intermarriage and commingling among these three groups, and ethnic allegiances in Bosnia had generally faded into the background. Still, Muslims were more inclined to regard themselves as Yugoslavs and, after the dissolution of Yugoslavia, as Bosnians.

The historical and emotional connections of Bosnian Serbs and Croats with the Serbian and Croatian republics remained, ready to be exploited by chauvinist politicians. The disappearance of Tito and Kardelj, the strongest personifications of Yugoslav nationalism, was particularly damaging to Bosnian solidarity. Tito's government, for nearly forty years, governed with restrained tolerance of ethnic and regional allegiances. The goal was to create a lasting national state. It was as if Tito and Kardelj had read the ideas of Simmel on the nature of ethnic dissociation and the need for conflict release devices in a multinational state.

Paradoxically, those very policies strengthened local republicanism, as did the economic and political decentralization occurring throughout the postwar period. This facilitated the ethnic nationalism that regional politicians such as Tudjman and Milosevic would ultimately use to dismantle the federal state and revive old intercommunal fears and resentment. This prepared the way for the wars of Slovenian, Croatian, and especially Bosnian secession.

### The Collapse of Federal Yugoslavia

One can regard Tito's Yugoslavia as a situation of potential conflict. His personal power, together with the political and economic structure his party created, kept that conflict from becoming overt until his death. Regional forces – religious, political, economic – were nevertheless already emerging in the 1970s. Local political elites hardly concealed their aspirations, and workers were increasingly disillusioned with an economy that was not working for them. Despite a reform movement, by the mid-1980s the foreign debt, industrial mismanagement, and triple-digit inflation were grinding Yugoslav nationalism into the ground, and "the republics gained enormous power and came to be identified in each case (except for Bosnia) with a particular national viewpoint" (Donia and Fine 1994, 199). A federal, integrated, multinational Yugoslavia was on the way out.

These decentralizing forces were further stimulated by the dissolution of socialist governments elsewhere in Europe. Long-dormant regional and ethnoreligious identities in Yugoslavia were about to be reawakened by newly elected republican governments in its various republics.

The escalation of conflict in Bosnia can be understood only as part of the larger collapse of Yugoslavia. Its events and dynamics were almost always a consequence of external intervention by Croatia and the Serb-run Federal Republic of Yugoslavia (consisting of Serbia and Montenegro), both continually seeking to expand their territories and consolidate their power; and by third parties (the UN, the European Union, NATO, the United States, and Russia). By the late 1980s, the three institutions holding Yugoslavia together were rapidly weakening: the federal presidency, the Communist Party, and the Yugoslav People's Army.

The first of these, the federal presidency, was weakened as party leaders, government officials, and territorial forces in the various republics were all acquiring power. For example, by 1987 a new leader, Milosevic, had taken control of the Serbian government, and in 1989 Serbia annexed the autonomous provinces of Kosovo and Vojvodina, thus getting closer to its dream of "Greater Serbia." The Croatian president Tudjman had similarly consolidated his power. Through such personal power accretion, the Serb and Croat leaders had made implicit commitments to their minorities outside their borders who aspired to inclusion in these new states.

The elections held in the individual republics from August through December 1990 brought to power new nationalist and separatist leaders nearly everywhere, thus showing that legitimacy and authority had shifted to the republics. Moreover, the scheduled Yugoslav national elections were never held. The new governments in Slovenia, Croatia, and Macedonia now judged that they had a mandate to consolidate their power by holding referenda proposing either a much looser Yugoslav confederation of sovereign republics or outright independence. The Serbian regime, too, was flush with new legitimacy from its elections, though Serbia-Montenegro wished to maintain the Yugoslav state in some form. Only Bosnia-Herzegovina supported continuation of the federal Yugoslavia Tito had created.

Because the governments of Croatia, the Federal Republic (Serbia-Montenegro), and Bosnia were the primary parties in the Bosnian conflict, one could say that by late 1991, with those parties in place, the conflict was rapidly emerging, on its way to escalation. As Slovenia was seceding in December 1991, Yugoslavia's last federal prime minister, a Croat, resigned. At that point, Tito's Yugoslavia had ceased to exist.

The second leg of Yugoslav legitimacy had been the Communist Party. Throughout the 1980s, its branches in the various republics had been resisting the policy of "democratic centralism" – a policy that demanded radical political and economic reform shifting more power toward local governments (Donia and Fine 1994, 206). However, once communism became discredited elsewhere in Europe, Communist Party organizations in the individual republics were fast remaking themselves. The Fourteenth (and last) Extraordinary Party Congress of January 1990 adjourned in turmoil. In subsequent elections in Croatia and the Federal Republic, party leaders gained control of those governments, thus further consolidating two of the three power levers in their own hands.

The third guarantor of Yugoslav integrity, the Yugoslav People's Army (YPA), had always been Serb-dominated and was the last to be transformed by the new leaders. In fact, its very existence depended on a united Yugoslavia's survival, because its officer corps had, from its creation, been of a decidedly Serbian complexion. Its loyalty was therefore largely to a Serbian Yugoslavia, to Belgrade. It had always been a heavily politicized force, and the dissolution of the League of Yugoslav Communists created much conflict and uncertainty, especially among its officers.

After its embarrassing failure to keep Slovenia in the federation, the YPA became – through purges, desertions, delegation of responsibility, and license to paramilitary Serb groups in Croatia and Bosnia – even more Serbian. At that point, it had shifted its strategy away from preserving Yugoslavia toward building a Greater Serbia. As it lost the status of a Yugoslav national army and was reorganized as a Serb force, the territorial forces of each republic became the military arms of their own governments. As new weapons purchases by Croatia in 1991 suggested, an arms race was under way. By that time, the ruling parties, governmental machinery, and military forces were consolidated in Croatia and the Federal Republic. Rather quickly, these power agencies became linked to ethnoreligious identities in Croatia, the Federal Republic, and Bosnia.

# Notes

## Chapter One: Introduction

1. To learn about this accumulated knowledge, see, for example, Deutsch (1973), Kriesberg ([1973] 1982; 1998), or Blalock (1989).
2. Third parties will not be considered as a part of the general theory discussed in Chapter 7. However, they will be considered in Chapter 8, when our theory is applied to the Bosnian conflict.

## Chapter Two: Understanding Conflict

1. For example, Himes (1980, 14) defines social conflict as "purposeful struggles between collective actors who use social power to defeat or remove opponents and to gain status, power, resources, and other scarce values"; Kriesberg ([1973] 1982, 17) says "conflict exists when two or more parties believe they have incompatible objectives"; Pruitt and Rubin (1986, 10) see conflict as "perceived divergence of interests"; Blalock (1989, 7) defines conflict as "intentional mutual exchange of negative sanctions."
2. Hence Pruitt and Rubin's (1986, 10) definition of conflict as a "perceived divergence of interests."
3. This may be why Blalock (1989, 7) defines conflict as "intentional mutual exchange of negative sanctions."
4. Formally, a logical contradiction is defined as a statement that asserts that both A and not-A are true.

5. Most of game-theoretical literature distinguishes between unobservable "utilities" and observable "payoffs." To simplify our terminology, we shall apply the term "payoffs" to both concepts.

6. When we say that, to the husband, having four children is worth −3 "points," we mean simply that, on some arbitrary scale, the husband's answers to the query were scored as −3.

7. In practice, we are seldom able to secure such exact numbers. Thus working with payoff matrices is primarily of theoretical interest: they help us to think systematically about conflicts.

8. The payoffs are assumed to be constructed in such a manner that any solution with a positive payoff is acceptable; but see note 12.

9. For a discussion of rational decision making, see Luce and Raiffa's (1967, chs. 13 and 14) analysis of individual and group decision making.

10. We speak here about "coercive" rather than "competitive" action because, as we just noted, competition is usually viewed as distinct from conflict.

11. Making a threat believable becomes a game in itself. It can be argued, for example, that one strategy is to show that a third party will administer the punishment without regard to what is beneficial to the players.

12. Throughout this book, we assume that the players do not accept negative payoffs. However, this assumption presupposes that the players can withdraw from the game and that the return to the "status quo" has zero payoff for them. When they can secure zero payoff by withdrawing, they will not accept negative payoff. In our illustration, however, the threat covers all possible outcomes short of having four children. The husband cannot return to the status quo by simply refusing to discuss the topic any further. If he tries to do so, his wife will leave him, so the "status quo" has even lower payoff for him $(0 - 10 = -10)$ than having four children, and he has to opt for the alternative with the highest negative payoff – having four children.

13. In some cases, the reward may come from a third party. For example, the United States, while mediating the conflict between the Israelis and the Palestinians, might promise substantial foreign aid to both sides if they agree to have Jerusalem governed by an international body.

14. Consider, for instance, the variable of "fear." When we view it as a continuous variable, we may assign numbers to it on a, say, 10-point scale, with 1 standing for "minimally afraid," 10 for "maximally afraid." But when we view it as a concept that can have only two categories, "afraid" and "not afraid," then we may have to say that a person who scales between 0 and 5 is "not afraid," one that scores between 5 and 10 is "afraid." This possibility, of course, leads to the same problem as in Figure 2.1.

## Chapter Three: Development of Incompatible Goals

1.  We sometimes advocate empowering the weak as if such an act did not disempower anybody. But close inspection of real-life cases suggests otherwise. For example, when a mediator tries to empower a tenant, the landlord will resist these attempts, knowing well that this would decrease his own power. It should be noted, however, that some writers, speaking about "power with" rather than "power over," argue that the supply of power can be expanded through cooperation, not simply reallocated.
2.  Homans gives somewhat different definitions at different points in his book. The definition given here is based on his summary statement (268) and seems to capture the essence of his theory.
3.  It could be argued that it is enough for one party to believe that it is treated unjustly. But it is also important whether injustice is an *objective fact*: conflicts in which one party's perceptions of injustice is not objectively supported are different from those in which their belief is factually correct. For example, a party that falsely believes itself to be treated unjustly may have difficulty in finding allies.
4.  Davis (1962, 5–19) called this the "revolution of rising expectations."
5.  Originally, the word "charisma" meant "grace of God."
6.  Weber ([1922] 1947) speaks about "rational-legal" authority, but the term "bureaucratic" seems more descriptive.
7.  At that time, the region that is now southern Arizona was ruled by Spain.
8.  Some related terms have different meanings. For example, "belligerency" often means being in a state of war. We do not give this concept that meaning.
9.  The most important functionalist was Talcott Parsons (see Parsons and Shills 1951).
10. The distinction between an "institution" and an "organization" is somewhat vague. Generally speaking, institutions are social arrangements, such as the family, that serve an important function in a manner sanctioned by tradition; organizations are arrangements with a clearly defined division of labor. Some groups may be viewed as both institutions and organizations. For example, a particular religious congregation may be seen as a religious institution because it serves functions such as social integration; it may also be seen as an organization because it has a division of labor that assigns different roles to specialists (the minister, the deacon, the altar boy, and so on).
11. How important land was for members of the European aristocracy is indicated by the fact that their family names generally designated the land

they owned, containing "von," "van," or "de" – all of which mean "from [a certain territory]."

12. For example, he noted that, contrary to Marx's predictions, revolutions occur at the beginning rather than at the end of a capitalist era.

13. For example, the U.S. government is based on a threefold separation of political power, while antitrust legislation seeks to limit concentration of economic power.

14. Dahrendorf's theory, although more general than Marx's, is also incomplete. For example, because he did not consider value differences as a possible source of conflict, he would be unable to explain why different ethnic groups in the former USSR were in conflict with each other.

15. Different tribes often try to maintain some interaction through intermarriage, but this custom is not sufficient to sustain the kind of interaction that creates common culture.

16. For example, Durkheim ([1893] 1964) spoke about mechanical and organic solidarity; Tönnies ([1887] 1963) about *Gemeinschaft* and *Gesellschaft*; Cooley (1902) about primary and secondary groups; Redfield (1941) about folk and urban societies.

17. An action is "instrumentally" rational when it has a specific goal and is preceded by a consideration of the available options and evaluation of their consequences, and when it aims at the option that emerges from this consideration as the best.

18. For an argument that postindustrial systems will promote quite different values than industrial systems, see Bartos (1996).

## Chapter Four: Application to the Civil Rights Struggle

1. An internal conflict occurs between parties who belong to the same group, organization, institution, or society. In most cases, it is due to oppression of a subordinate group by a powerful group; but, as we saw, it can also involve equals who play different roles or have different values.

2. For example, if we were attempting to minimize violence in the civil rights struggle, we might "go from left to right" and note that a sense of injustice leads to goal incompatibility (which, in turn, may erupt into open conflict). And we thus might try to minimize injustice.

3. Contested resources are a "direct" cause of goal incompatibility because the arrow from resources to incompatibility does not go through any other variable.

4. For an analysis of the first year of civil rights sit-ins, see Wehr (1968).

5. If we were to consider strife within an organization, such as General Motors, we might ask whether the two racial groups played different roles in that organization. Because we are considering a nationwide conflict, we must limit our consideration to organizations that include, at least in principle, all U.S. citizens. And the U.S. government is such an organization.

## Chapter Five: Emergence of Overt Conflicts

1. Dahrendorf discussed some additional conditions, but these are the most important (Johnson 1981, 472).
2. When interaction is not free, these consequences might not occur. For example, communication between a master and his slave seldom creates friendship between the two.
3. Because the arrow is double-headed, it indicates mutual influences. The expression "vice versa" means that the arrow linking interaction and similarity can be also interpreted as "The more similar the members, the more they will interact with each other."
4. Once again, remember that the ideas of the leaders carry disproportionately heavy weight.
5. Note that persons play dual theoretical roles: on one hand, they are viewed as interacting individuals who contribute to conflict solidarity; on the other hand, they are viewed as a resource.
6. The Japanese attack on Pearl Harbor was viewed as illegal because it occurred before war was declared.

## Chapter Six: Application to a University Conflict

1. Exogenous causes are without arrows leading *into* them. In our figures, exogenous causes are located at the extreme left of the figure.
2. The Chicano faculty members were on the fringes of two groups without being fully accepted by either: on one hand, they felt that they were not fully accepted by the university establishment; on the other, they were open to criticism by the Chicano community for not fighting energetically enough for Chicano interests.
3. This is because "incompatibility" is a concept that expresses the relationship between the two sides of a conflict.
4. As our discussion in Chapter 7 shows, the theory of escalation considers primarily how a party reacts to opponent's coercive action.
5. Negotiation and mediation will be considered in Chapter 9.

## Chapter Seven: Escalation and Deescalation

1. The one exception is Simmel ([1908] 1955). But even he did not go far beyond noting that conflicts tend to increase group solidarity.

2. For reasons discussed later, the model deals with unilateral *dee*scalation $-u$P rather than unilateral escalation $+u$P.

3. Because an increase in Opponent's coerciveness (an increase in O) will increase Party's escalation (an increase dP/dt), we may say that $r$O represents reciprocated escalation.

4. The term dP/dt is used in differential equations. It refers to the change in P (dP) over an infinitely small interval of time (dt).

5. This interpretation of $r$ is somewhat oversimplified. More exactly, $r$ specifies how much of the Party's escalation (dP/dt) is due to Opponent's coerciveness (O).

6. When $h$ is a negative number, it stands for "friendliness."

7. The assumption that parameters do not change is somewhat complex. See, for example, Leik and Meeker (1975, 5).

8. The equations 7.1 contain a feedback from the opponent's action to that of the party.

9. The terminology used here is somewhat different from that used by Richardson.

10. As is customary, the equations 7.1 assume that all three parameters are positive. But when that is assumed, using a positive term $+u$P would make all three terms on the right-hand side of 7.1 positive – and escalation would never stop! Thus *something* must be able to curb escalation, and the negative term $-u$P performs that function.

11. A conflict is in an equilibrium if the adversaries retain the same level of coerciveness.

12. Two adversaries are considered here to be "similar" if they have the same parameters $r$, $u$, and $h$.

13. Regrettably, the fact that unilateral action is designated by a *negative* expression $-u$P can create confusion. But the fact is that, when $-u$P is used, a large value of $u$ means that Party *dee*scalates powerfully.

14. Some may argue that stable peace can be obtained even when the parties continue coercing each other, providing they do it in a nonviolent way. Clearly, our conclusion does not hold for that view.

15. This conclusion is obvious from equation 7.3: $P^* = O^* = 0$ cannot be obtained by adjusting $u$ or $r$ – only by setting $h = 0$.

16. Because we are considering the simplifying case when the parameters of the two adversaries are identical, and are assuming that they reached a stalemate, their level of coerciveness will be the same, $P = O$. Thus we may

substitute P for O, and equations 7.1 may be rewritten as

$$dP/dt = rP - uP + h = (r - u)P + h$$

Because we are assuming (in equations 7.2) that $u$ is larger than $r$, and since P remains positive (i.e., coercive behavior is still taking place), the expression $(r - u)$ P will be negative. And deescalation will be taking place as long as $(r - u)$ P is smaller than $h$ or, alternately, as long as $(u - r)$ P is larger than $h$:

$$(u - r)\,P > h$$

But, obviously, as deescalation progresses, P is getting smaller, and in order for this inequality to hold, at least one of the following must happen: tendency to retaliate $r$ must grow smaller, tendency to curb escalation unilaterally $u$ must grow larger, or hostility $h$ must grow smaller.

17. It is clear from the equilibrium equation that it is impossible to choose $u$ or $r$ in such a manner that P* and O* become zero. True, it is possible for the expression $(u - r)$ to become negative, thus making P* and O* negative as well. But, as Figure 7.2 illustrates, this leads to runaway escalation.

18. While explaining our model, we assumed that the adversaries had the same action propensities ($u$, $r$, and $h$). But this was only a simplifying assumption made to facilitate our discussion. In the real world, the adversaries usually have different action propensities.

19. NATO's claims of its bombing effectiveness in the Kosovo conflict have been challenged as hollow and misleading (see Barry and Thomas 2000).

20. For an alternative to the official narrative on the rationale for using the bomb, see Lifton and Mitchell (1996).

21. This feedback is not shown in Figure 7.3.

22. See Wehr (1968, 67–69) for an analysis of protester motivation.

## Chapter Eight: Application to Conflict in Bosnia

1. For an excellent summary account of the Bosnian war, see Kaldor (1999).

2. See the census data reported in Donia and Fine (1994, 86–87).

3. As the theory of Chapter 3 suggests, most conflicts involve incompatible goals. However, conflicts can also start because of mutual hostility.

4. That the Bosnian government agreed most reluctantly, and that the Federal Republic of Yugoslavia (Serbia-Montenegro) had to initial the agreement for Bosnian Serb leaders, only later "coaxing" their signatures, suggested the difficulty that lay ahead in implementing the agreement and rebuilding a multiethnic Bosnia.

5. That the threat to Serb Forces was real is shown by the fact that, by summer 1994, Bosnian forces reached 110,000 (Rogel 1998, 32).

6. Recall that, at that point, Serbs engaged in coerciveness of a different kind, ethnic cleansing.

7. This promise was implied when the UN force was reduced from 12,500 to 5,000 and when it was renamed, indicating that its mission was a mere "confidence restoration" (Rogel 1998, 37).

8. Figure 8.5 is simplified because it does not display some of the variables shown in Figures 8.2 and 8.5: it omits the earlier version's exogenous variables (such as dissolution of Yugoslavia) and intervening variables (such as conflict organization). It augments Figure 8.4 by considering conflict escalation and its three components – unilateral escalation, reciprocation, and hostility.

## Chapter Nine: Making Conflict Work Economically

1. An "I message" always begins with "I" and continues on to express a state of emotion or belief such as "I feel that we are not understanding … " This form of speaking locates the ownership of the statement clearly with the speaker, and thus tends to reduce blaming the listener, reveals the speaker's wish to communicate clearly, and encourages a similar direct and revealing communication from the listener.

2. In the terminology of our Chapter 3, this means that instead of discussing the "labels" of the payoff matrix (e.g., "We want the wage of $20"), the negotiators should speak about their payoffs and the underlying outcomes (e.g., "We need higher wages because of the increased cost of living").

3. Goffman has been criticized for advocating manipulation and insincere playacting. We believe that, to be a skilled negotiator, one does not merely pretend to be conciliatory, powerful, and fair; that one in fact is all of these.

4. For a formal proof that such a procedure is fair, see Nash (1950) or Bartos (1967).

5. These distinctions are closely related to the distinctions between three types of conflict action we discussed in Chapter 2: coercion, persuasion, and reward.

6. Coleman discusses here only one type of tit-for-tat behavior, the exchange of punishing behaviors. Because, in Chapter 7, we discussed a tit-for-tat strategy that also involves exchanges of rewarding behavior and *unilateral* rewarding moves, its consequences tend to be beneficial to both sides.

7. To repeat, Coleman does not refer here to the tit-for-tat strategy we discussed in Chapter 7. That strategy advocates not only symmetric reciprocation but also asymmetric (unilateral) cooperation.

8. As we have noted on several occasions, rational decisions can be reached only if the decision makers take time to consider carefully their options, the consequences of each option, and the "payoff" of consequence has for them.

## Chapter Ten: Understanding and Managing Conflicts

1. Because hostility can contribute to conflict as much as goal incompatibility, perhaps we should have given both concepts equal treatment. But we did not consider hostility in the same detailed fashion primarily because it can be explained rather simply: as shown in Figure 5.2, it is due either to grievances or frustration.

2. Remember that Party may be said to reciprocate if its escalation is roughly of the same size as Opponent's last escalation; it is said to retaliate if its escalation is larger.

3. See, for example, Mitchell's (1993, 147) list of different intervenor types and functions required to resolve a complex civil conflict.

# References

Aho, James. 1994. *This Thing of Darkness*. Seattle: University of Washington Press.

Arendt, Hannah. 1965. *On Revolution*. New York: Viking.

Axelrod, Robert. 1984. *The Evolution of Cooperation*. New York: Basic Books.

Bacharach, Samuel, and Edward J. Lawler. 1981. *Power and Politics in Organizations*. San Francisco: Jossey-Bass.

Barry, John, and Evan Thomas. 2000. The Kosovo cover-up. *Newsweek*, May 15.

Bartos, Otomar J. 1967. *Simple Models of Group Behavior*. New York: Columbia University Press.

Bartos, Otomar J. 1989. Agreement in mediation. *Peace and Change*, no. 14: 425–443.

Bartos, Otomar J. 1996. Postmodernism, postindustrialism, and the future. *Sociological Inquiry* 37 (2): 307–325.

Bellah, Robert N., R. Madsen, W. M. Sullivan, A. Swidler, and S. M. Tipton. 1986. *Habits of the Heart*. New York: Harper & Row.

Berelson, Bernard, and Gart A. Steiner. 1964. *Human Behavior: An Inventory of Scientific Findings*. New York: Harcourt, Brace & World.

Berger, Peter, and Thomas Luckman. 1966. *The Social Construction of Reality*. New York: Anchor.

Blalock, Hubert M. 1989. *Power and Conflict*. Newbury Park, CA: Sage.

Blau, Peter M. 1964. *Exchange and Power in Social Life*. New York: Wiley.

Bogan, Denitch. 1994. *Ethnic Nationalism: The Tragic Death of Yugoslavia*. Minneapolis: University of Minnesota Press.

Bondurant, Joan. 1988. *Conquest of Violence*. Princeton, NJ: Princeton University Press.

Boulding, Kenneth. 1988. *Conflict and Defense*. Lanham, MD: University Press of America.

Boulding, Kenneth. 1989. *Three Faces of Power*. Newbury Park, CA: Sage.

Branch, Taylor. 1988. *Parting of the Waters*. New York: Simon and Schuster.

Brinton, Crane. 1955. *The Anatomy of Revolution*. New York: Vintage.

Burgess, Guy, Heidi Burgess, and Paul Wehr. 1998. Confronting and managing resolution-resistant conflicts. *<www.usip.org>*.

Burgess, Heidi, and Guy Burgess. 1997. *Encyclopedia of Conflict Resolution*. Santa Barbara, CA: ABC-Clio.

Burton, John. 1969. *Conflict and Communication*. London: Macmillan.

Burton, John. 1990. *Conflict Resolution and Provention*. London: Macmillan.

Busch, Robert Baruch, and Joseph Folger. 1994. *The Promise of Mediation*. San Francisco: Jossey-Bass.

Carnegie Commission on Preventing Deadly Conflict. 1997. *Preventing Deadly Conflict*. New York: Carnegie Corporation.

Chasin, Richard, Margaret Herzig, Sallyann Roth, Laura Chasin, Carol Becker, and Robert Stains Jr. 1996. From diatribe to dialogue on divisive public issues. *Mediation Quarterly* 13 (4): 323–344.

Christenson, Reo M., Alan S. Engel, Dan N. Jacobs, Mostafa Rejai, and Herbert Waltzer. 1975. *Ideologies and Modern Politics*. New York: Dodd, Mead.

Christie, Daniel, Richard Wagner, and Deborah Winger, eds. 2001. *Peace, Conflict, and Violence: Peace Psychology for the 21st Century*. Upper Saddle River, NJ: Prentice-Hall.

Clark, Howard. 2000. *Civil Resistance in Kosovo*. London: Pluto.

Coleman, James. 1957. *Community Conflict*. New York: Free Press.

Collins, Randall. 1988. *Theoretical Sociology*. New York: Harcourt Brace Jovanovich.

Collins, Randall. 1992. *Sociological Insight*. New York: Oxford University Press.

Cooley, Charles Horton. 1902. *Human Nature and Social Order*. New York: Scribner.

*COPRED*. 2000. *Global Directory of Peace Studies and Conflict Resolution Programs*. COPRED, The Evergreen State College, Seminar 3127. Olympia, WA 98505. <copred@evergreen.edu>.

Coser, Lewis A. 1956. *The Functions of Social Conflict*. New York: Free Press.

Crnobrnja, Mihailo. 1994. *The Yugoslav Drama*. Montreal: McGill-Queens University Press.

Curle, Adam. 1971. *Making Peace*. London: Tavistock.

Dahrendorf, Ralf. 1959. *Class and Class Conflict in Industrial Society.* Stanford, CA: Stanford University Press.

Davis, James. 1962. Toward a theory of revolution. *American Sociological Review* 27: 5–18.

Deutsch, Morton. 1973. *The Resolution of Conflict: Constructive and Destructive Processes.* New Haven, CT: Yale University Press.

Deutsch, Morton, and Peter T. Coleman, eds. 2000. *The Handbook of Conflict Resolution: Theory and Practice.* San Francisco: Jossey-Bass.

Dollard, John, Leonard W. Doob, Neal E. Miller, O. H. Mowrer, and Robert R. Sears. 1939. *Frustration and Aggression.* New Haven, CT: Yale University Press.

Donia, Robert, and John Fine Jr. 1994. *Bosnia and Hercegovina: A Tradition Betrayed.* New York: Columbia University Press.

Doob, Leonard, and W. J. Foltz. 1974. The impact of a workshop on grass roots leaders in Belfast. *Journal of Conflict Resolution* 18 (2): 237–256.

Downton, James, Jr., and Paul Wehr. 1997. *The Persistent Activist.* Boulder, CO: Westview.

Dubois, W. E. B. 1899. *The Philadelphia Negro.* Philadelphia: University of Pennsylvania Press.

Durkheim, Émile. [1893] 1964. *The Division of Labor in Society.* New York: Macmillan.

Etzioni, Amitai. 1962. *The Hard Way to Peace.* New York: Collier.

Fisher, Roger. 1970. *International Conflict for Beginners.* New York: Harper and Row.

Fisher, Roger, and William Ury. 1981. *Getting to Yes.* Boston: Houghton-Mifflin.

Frazier, E. Franklin. 1962. *The Black Bourgeoisie.* New York: Collier.

Gamson, William. 1990. *The Strategy of Social Protest.* Belmont, CA: Wadsworth.

Goffman, Erving. 1967. *Interaction Ritual.* Chicago: Aldine.

Goffman, Erving. 1974. *Frame Analysis.* Cambridge, MA: Harvard University Press.

Griffin-Nolan, Edward. 1991. *Witness for Peace.* Louisville, KY: Westminster/ John Knox.

Gurr, Ted R. 1970. *Why Men Rebel.* Princeton, NJ: Princeton University Press.

Habermas, Jürgen. 1987. *The Theory of Communicative Action.* Vol. 2: *Lifeworld and System.* Boston: Beacon Press.

Hall, Richard H. 1982. *Organizations: Structure and Process.* Englewood Cliffs, NJ: Prentice-Hall.

Hechter, Michael. 1987. *Principles of Group Solidarity*. Berkeley: University of California Press.

Himes, Joseph S. 1980. *Conflict and Conflict Management*. Athens: University of Georgia Press.

Hocker, Joyce, and William Wilmot. 1991. *Interpersonal Conflict*. Dubuque, IA: Wiliam C. Brown.

Holbrooke, Richard. 1998. *To End a War*. New York: Random House.

Homans, George C. 1950. *The Human Group*. New York: Harcourt.

Homans, George C. 1974. *Social Behavior: Its Elementary Forms*. New York: Harcourt.

Ignatieff, Michael. 1997. *The Warrior's Honor*. New York: Henry Holt.

Johnson, Doyle P. 1981. *Sociological Theory*. New York: Wiley.

Jones, Ellis, Ross HaenFler, and Brett Johnson with Brian Klocke. 2001. *The Better World Handbook: From Good Intentions to Everyday Actions*. Gabriola Island, BC: New Society Publishers.

Kaldor, Mary. 1999. *New and Old Wars*. Stanford, CA: Stanford University Press.

Karis, Thomas, and Gail M. Gerhart. 1977. *Challenge and Violence, 1953–1964*. Volume 3 of Thomas Karis and Gwendolyn M. Carter, eds., *From Protest to Challenge: A Documentary History of African Politics in South Africa*. Stanford, CA: Hoover Institution Press.

Karis, Thomas, and Gail M. Gerhart. 1997. *Nadir and Resurgence, 1964–1979*. Volume 5 of Thomas Karis and Gwendolyn M. Carter, eds., *From Protest to Challenge: A Documentary History of African Politics in South Africa*. Bloomington: Indiana University Press.

Kelman, Herbert. 1982. Creating conditions for Israeli-Palestinian negotiations. *Journal of Conflict Resolution*. 26 (1): 39–76.

Kennedy Robert. 1969. *Thirteen Days: A Memoir of the Cuban Missile Crisis*. New York: Norton.

Kolb, Deborah. 1995. *When Talk Works*. San Francisco: Jossey-Bass.

Kriesberg, Louis. [1973] 1982. *Social Conflicts*. Englewood Cliffs, NJ: Prentice-Hall.

Kriesberg, Louis. 1998. *Constructive Conflicts*. New York: Rowman & Little-field.

Lederach, John Paul. 1997. *Building Peace: Sustainable Reconciliation in Divided Societies*. Washington, DC: United States Institute of Peace.

Lederach, John Paul. 1999. *The Journey toward Reconciliation*. Scottsdale, PA: Herald Press.

Leik, Robert K., and Barbara F. Meeker. 1975. *Mathematical Sociology*. Englewood Cliffs, NJ: Prentice-Hall.

Lifton, Robert Jay, and Greg Mitchell. 1996. *Hiroshima in America*. New York: Avon.

Light, Donald, Jr., and Suzanne Keller. 1979. *Sociology*. New York: Knopf.

Luce, R. Duncan, and Howard Raiffa. 1967. *Games and Decisions*. New York: Wiley.

Lulofs, Roxane S., and Dudley D. Cahn. 2000. *Conflict: From Theory to Action*. Boston: Allyn & Bacon.

Luthuli, Albert. 1962. *Let My People Go*. New York: McGraw-Hill.

Mahony, Liam, and Luis Eguren. 1997. *Unarmed Bodyguards*. West Hartford, CT: Kumarian.

Malinowski, Bronislaw. 1948. *Magic, Science and Religion, and Other Essays*. Glencoe, IL: Free Press.

Manis, Jerome G. 1984. *Serious Social Problems*. Boston: Allyn & Bacon.

Marx, Karl. [1867,1885,1894] 1967. *Capital*. 3 vols. Translated by S. Moore and E. Aveling. New York: International Publishers.

Marx, Karl, and Frederick Engels. [1846] 1947. *The German Ideology*. New York: International Publishers.

McAdam, Doug. 1982. *Political Process and the Development of Black Insurgency, 1930–1970*. Chicago: University of Chicago Press.

McAdam, Doug. 1988. *Freedom Summer: The Idealists Revisited*. New York: Oxford University Press.

Melucci, Alberto. 1980. The new social movements: A theoretical approach. *Social Science Information* 19: 199–226.

Miall, Hugh, Oliver Ramsbotham, and Tom Woodhouse. 1999. *Contemporary Conflict Resolution*. Cambridge: Polity.

Mitchell, Christopher. 1993. The process and stages of mediation: The Sudanese cases. In D. Smock, ed., *Making War and Waging Peace*, 147. Washington, DC: United States Institute of Peace.

Mitchell, Christopher, and Michael Banks. 1996. *Handbook of Conflict Resolution*. London: Pinter.

Moore, Christopher. 1986. *The Mediation Process*. San Francisco: Jossey-Bass.

Morgan, M. P. 1977. *Deterrence: A Conceptual Analysis*. Beverly Hills, CA: Sage.

Morgenthau, Hans. 1960. *Politics among Nations*. New York: Knopf.

Morris, Aldon. 1984. *Origins of the Civil Rights Movement*. New York: Free Press.

Murray, Ruppert. 1997. *IFOR on IFOR: NATO Peacekeeping in Bosnia Herzegovina*. Conshohocken, PA: Combined Publishing.

Myrdal, Gunnar. 1944. *An American Dilemma*. New York: Harper.

Nash, John F. 1950. The bargaining problem. *Econometrica* 18: 155–162.

Nepstad, Sharon Erickson. 1997. The process of cognitive liberation. *Sociological Inquiry* 67 (4): 470–487.

Nepstad, Sharon Erickson. 2001. Constructing transnational solidarity. *Mobilization* 6 (1).

Olson, Mancur, Jr. 1965. *The Logic of Collective Action.* New York: Schocken Books.

Osgood, Charles. 1962. *Alternative to War or Surrender.* Urbana: University of Illinois Press.

Owen, David. 1995. *Balkan Odyssey.* New York: Harcourt Brace.

Park, Robert E., and Ernest W. Burgess. 1921. *Introduction to the Science of Sociology.* Chicago: University of Chicago Press.

Parsons, Talcott. 1977. *The Evolution of Societies.* Englewood Cliffs, NJ: Prentice-Hall.

Parsons, Talcott, and Robert Bales. 1955. *Family, Socialization, and Interaction Process.* New York: Free Press.

Parsons, Talcott, and Edward A. Shills, eds. 1951. *Toward a General Theory of Action.* New York: Harper & Row.

Parsons, Talcott, and Neil M. Smelser. 1956. *Economy and Society.* Glencoe, IL: Free Press.

Patfoort, Pat. 1995. *Uprooting Violence.* Freeport, ME: Cobblesmith Press.

Patfoort, Pat. 2001. *I Want, You Don't Want: Nonviolence Education.* Freeport, ME: Cobblesmith Press.

Porter, Jack N., and Ruth Taplin. 1987. *Conflict and Conflict Resolution.* Lanham, MD: University Press of America.

Pruitt, Dean G., and Jeffrey Z. Rubin. 1986. *Social Conflict: Escalation, Stalemate, and Settlement.* New York: Random House.

Ramet, Sabrina. 1996. *Balkan Babel: The Disintegration of Yugoslavia from the Death of Tito to Ethnic War.* Boulder CO: Westview.

Rapoport, Anatol. [1960] 1961. *Fights, Games and Debates.* Ann Arbor: University of Michigan Press.

Redfield, Robert. 1941. *The Folk Culture of Yucatan.* Chicago: University of Chicago Press.

Richardson, Lewis F. 1960. *Arms and Insecurity.* Pittsburgh: Boxwood.

Ritzer, George. 1992. *Contemporary Sociological Theory.* New York: McGraw-Hill.

Rogel, Carol. 1998. *The Breakup of Yugoslavia and the War in Bosnia.* Westport, CT: Greenwood Press.

Rohrbaugh, John, and Paul Wehr. 1978. Judgment analysis in policy formation: A new method for improving public participation. *Public Opinion Quarterly* 42 (4): 521–532.

Salert, Barbara, and F. Sprague. 1980. *The Dynamics of Riots*. Ann Arbor, MI: Inter-University Consortium for Political and Social Research.

Schoenhaus, Robert. 2001. *Conflict Management Training: Advancing Best Practices*. Washington, DC: United States Institute of Peace.

Sherif, Muzafer. 1936. The formation of a norm in a group situation. In M. Sherif, *The Psychology of Social Norms*. New York: Harper & Row.

Simmel, Georg. [1908] 1955. *Conflict and the Web of Group-Affiliations*. Translated by K. H. Wolff and R. Bendix. New York: Free Press.

Snow, David, and Robert Benford. 1988. Ideology, frame resonance, and participant mobilization. In Bert Klandermans, Hanspeter Kriesi, and Sidney Tarrow, eds., *International Social Movements Research*, 1:187–217. Greenwich, CT: JAI Press.

Sommer, Henrik. 1998. Non-Violent Direct Action: The Cycle of Protest and the Demise of Apartheid, 1970–94. Ph.D. dissertation, University of Colorado.

Stouffer, Samuel A., E. A. Suchman, L. C. DeVinney, S. A. Star, and R. M. Williams. 1949. *The American Soldier*. Princeton, NJ: Princeton University Press.

Sweeney, Edwin R. 1991. *Cochise*. Norman, OK: University of Oklahoma Press.

Thomas, William I. 1923. *The Unadjusted Girl*. Boston: Little & Brown.

Tillett, Gregory. 1991. *Resolving Conflict*. Sydney: Sydney University Press.

Tönnies, Ferdinand. [1887] 1963. *Community and Society*. New York: Harper & Row.

Ury, William. 1993. *Getting Past No*. New York: Bantam.

Ury, William, Jeanne Brett, and Stephen Goldberg. 1993. *Getting Disputes Resolved: Designing Systems to Cut the Costs of Conflict*. San Francisco: Jossey-Bass.

Walton, Jennifer G. 1970. Correlates of Coerciveness and Permissiveness of National Political Systems. Master's thesis, San Diego State College.

Walton, Richard, and Robert B. McKersie. 1965. *A Behavioral Theory of Labor Negotiations*. New York: McGraw-Hill.

Weber, Max. [1922] 1947. *The Theory of Social and Economic Organization*. New York: Oxford University Press.

Weber, Max. 1946. *From Max Weber: Essays in Sociology*. Edited by Hans Gerth and C. Wright Mills. New York: Oxford University Press.

*Webster's New Collegiate Dictionary*. 1976. Springfield, MA: Merriam.

Wehr, Paul. 1968. Nonviolence and differentiation in the equal rights movement. *Sociological Inquiry* 38 (1): 65–76.

Wehr, Paul. 1979. *Conflict Regulation*. Boulder, CO: Westview.

Wehr, Paul. 1985. Conflict and restraint: Poland, 1980–1982. In Peter Wallensteen, Johan Galtung, and Carlos Portales., eds., *Global Militarization*, 191–218. Boulder, CO: Westview Press.

Wehr, Paul. 1996. The citizen intervenor. *Peace Review* 8 (4): 555–561.

Wehr, Paul, and John Rohrbaugh. 1978. Citizen values and forest policy-making. *Western Sociological Review* 9 (1): 39–48.

Wehr, Paul, Heidi Burgess, and Guy Burgess, eds. 1994. *Justice without Violence.* Boulder, CO: Lynne Rienner Publishers.

Wehr, Paul, and John P. Lederach. 1991. Mediating conflict in Central America. *Journal of Peace Research* 28 (1): 85–98.

Wehr, Paul, and Sharon Nepstad. 1994. Violence, nonviolence and justice in Sandinista Nicaragua. In Paul Wehr, Heidi Burgess, and Guy Burgess, eds., *Justice without Violence*, 81–98. Boulder, CO: Lynne Rienner Publishers.

Western, Jon, and Daniel Serwer. 2000. *Bosnia's Next Five Years: Dayton and Beyond.* Washington, DC: United States Institute of Peace.

Wilson, William Julius. 1996. *When Work Disappears.* New York: Knopf.

Woods, Donald. 1987. *Biko.* New York: Henry Holt.

Yarrow, C. H. Mike. 1978. *Quaker Experience in International Conciliation.* New Haven, CT: Yale University Press.

Yevsukova, Marya. 1997. The theories of Georg Simmel and Lewis Coser Applied to Ethnic Conflict in Yugoslavia. Master's thesis, University of Colorado.

Zartman, William I., Daniel Druckman, Lloyd Jensen, Dean G. Pruitt, and H. Peyton Young. 1996. Negotiation is a search for justice. *International Negotiation* 1 (1): 79–98.

# Index